THE JOURNEY OF *Alvar Nuñez Cabeza de Vaca*

TRANSLATED FROM HIS
OWN NARRATIVE
BY FANNY BANDELIER

1734 East 71st Place, Chicago 49, Illinois

First edition from which
this printing was reproduced
was supplied by
INTERNATIONAL BOOKFINDERS
Box 3003
Beverly Hills, Calif.

A RIO GRANDE CLASSIC
First published in 1905

LIBRARY OF CONGRESS CARD CATALOG
64-15127

1964

1734 East 71st Place, Chicago 49, Illinois

INTRODUCTION

Of all the strange and wonderful stories that the discovery and exploration of the New World produced, there is none for sheer courage and struggle for survival against long odds that can compare with the tale of Alvar Núñez Cabeza de Vaca. His account of eight years of wanderings in the North American interior is the prototype and the masterpiece of this genre of true adventure. The early date and the circumstances of the shipwreck of the stragglers of Pánfilo de Nárvaez's ill-fated colonization expedition permitted Núñez Cabeza de Vaca to start the series of adventures for which he is justly famous. Through no fault or planning of his own, he was to become the first white man to play a significant role in the history of the American Southwest and the North Mexican states.

In his pedestrian activities this early Spanish explorer became the first to cross the North American continent from east to west in an area where the continental land mass spreads out to its standard width. In this regard it should be noted that his was not the first crossing of North America, as has often been claimed, since the lieutenants and rivals of Cortés had achieved this feat in central Mexico on numerous occasions. Even the distinction of being the first to visit the Río Grande eluded this accidental discoverer of many of the other geographical features of the Spanish Borderlands. In 1519, Alonso Alvarez de Piñeda had added the credit for discovering the Río Grande to his feat of having first seen the Mississippi River.

Though Alvar Núñez Cabeza de Vaca in his itinerary skirted the Buffalo Plains, he was the first to describe that shaggy inhabitant thereof, commenting on its utility and distribution. On three occasions he had seen the buffalo, and had the opportunity of eating the meat of these "cows."

In many other regards the former treasurer of Nărvaez's Florida endeavor became the first. His accounts stimulated a great impetus for interior exploration looking for fabulous cities that he had not seen, but the existence of which was reported by local Indian informants. The clever Andalusian was the first to see many of the Indian groups of the Borderlands, the first to introduce certain European culture elements and attitudes to these Indians, and the first to borrow native ideas and skills from the local aborigines in his efforts to survive. Núñez Cabeza de Vaca and his companions were the first to cross the wide expanses of what is today Texas. Modern historians doubt seriously whether the peripatetic Spaniard ever set foot in New Mexico, or any other of the United States, but he certainly crossed the Río Pecos and Río Grande not far from the present international border. Chihuahua and Sonora, among the North Mexican states, have the distinction of having him as their first visitor from among the Europeans.

Equally important with his unusual wanderings, was the fact that Alvar Núñez Cabeza de Vaca was a literate, urbane and engaging story teller. The usual result of a lone man fighting against tremendous odds, or of a small group of individuals attempting to avert the disaster that seems to surround them, is that despite heroic efforts they succumb to their fate. Thus we have no account of their activities. Once in a great while there is a little known survivor of great danger and long periods of privation, the story of a person cut off from all contact with civilization. Such persons are exemplified by Gerónimo Aguilar in Mexico, Juan Artiz in Florida, Caramarú in Brazil. Rarest of all are those few cases where the man or group of men possess the ability to transmit in prose some of the feeling of utter frustration, of terror of the unknown, of apprehension lest they become the next meal for their equally suspicious hosts, and of the strategems necessary to preserve life. Alexander Selkirk, shipwrecked on Juan Fernández Island off the Chilean coast, seems to possess some of the same elements of desperation, of adventure, and of final triumph. But the circumstances of Núñez Cabeza de Vaca's adventure and those of the inspiration for Daniel Defoe's fictional Robinson Crusoe are too divergent to merit comparison.

The dates of birth and death of our protaonist are as yet obscure. Born around 1490 in Jérez de la Frontera, between Cádiz and Sevilla, he was the first son of a prominent family, important on the maternal as well as the paternal side of the family. Alvar made frequent use of the maternal title, Cabeza de Vaca, which had been given to an early forebear who had assisted King Sancho of Navarre in the climactic battle of the Navas de Tolosa (1212) during the reconquest of Spain from the Moors. A strategic pass in the mountains had been marked for use by placing the skull of a cow at the entrance. The peasant sheepherder who performed this service was rewarded with the noble title of Cabeza de Vaca, or Cow's Head.

After several military campaigns in his youth, Alvar Núñez became a resident of Sevilla, the regional capital of Andalusia and point of departure for persons going to the New World. In 1527, he joined the Narvaez expedition which was staging in Sevilla for departure to Florida. Little did Cabeza de Vaca suspect that he was soon to participate in one of history's truly unique adventures.

The circumstances of the writing of Alvar Núñez Cabeza de Vaca's activities have a historical drawback in that the entire account was composed after his return to civilization in 1536. As a castaway, then successively as a slave, as a trader, or even as a medicine man and itinerant dignitary there was obviously very little opportunity or inclination for the Andalusian explorer to make notes, to preserve records, or in any way to keep track of his adventures, except mentally. His companions of the trail, Andrés Dorantes, Alonso del Castillo and the Moorish Estevanico, who aided in the successful outcome of the prolonged journey, also helped in recreating the events. The latter, sometimes called "Little Stephen," has frequently been identified as a Negro, but this seems to be the result of the same confusion of ethnic thinking that has made a Negro of Shakespeare's Othello.

Upon return to Spain, a 1542 edition of Cabeza de Vaca's *Los Naufragios* (The Castaways) was published in Zamora. This was followed in turn by a 1555 edition at nearby Valladolid. Between the dates of these two publications Alvar Núñez spent an unfortunate and unsuccessful term as governor of the Spanish possessions in the Río de la Plata area of South America. The second of the two early editions therefore contained an account of these later misadventures entitled *Comentarios de Alvar Núñez Cabeza de Vaca, Adelantado y Gobernador del Río de la Plata.* In due time Italian, French, German and English translations or paraphrases were available of one or both of Cabeza de Vaca's writings.

It would be surprising if the Cabeza de Vaca theme had been neglected by historians. Such has obviously not been the case. A dramatic and heroic character of his standing has had a long and distinguished bibliography of works concerning his adventures, particularly books published in Spain. His *Naufragios* has been repeatedly reprinted in Spain, but in English there has been less activity.

An early defective translation by Buckingham Smith appeared in 1851, which was re-edited by John Gilmary Shea in 1871. These translations were made from the 1555 or Valladolid edition. The same item appeared again

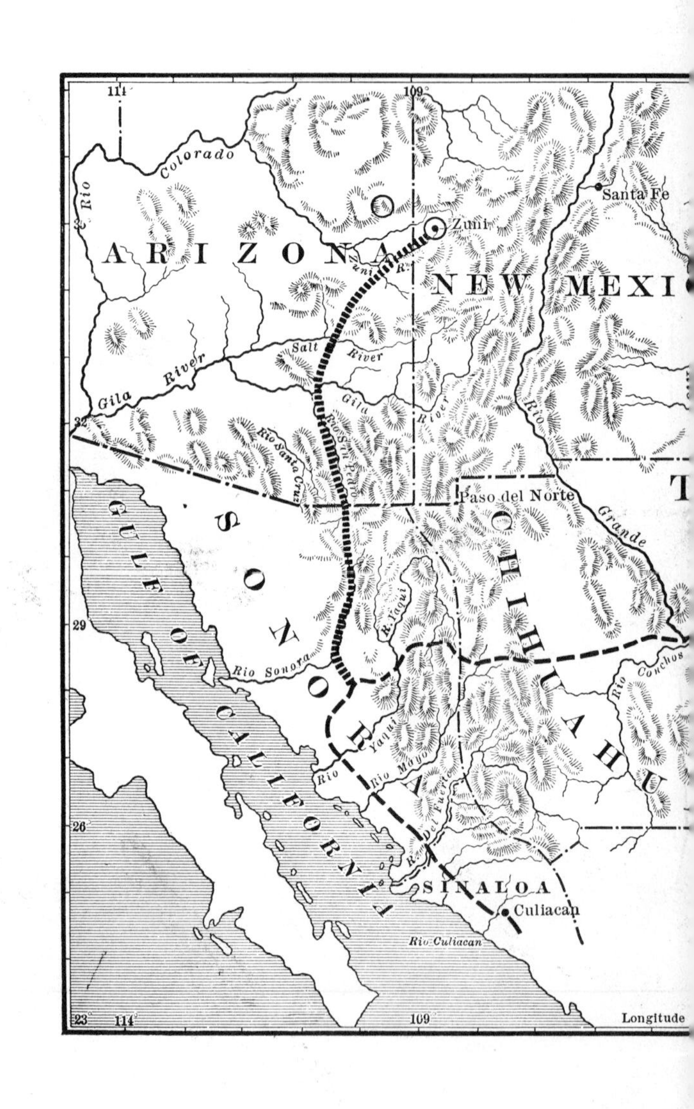

114°
109°
Rio Colorado
Santa Fe
Zuni
ARIZONA
Zuni R.
NEW MEXI
Salt River
Gila River
Gila River
Rio Santa Cruz
Rio San Pedro
Rio Grande
Paso del Norte
T
SONORA
CHIHUAHU
GULF OF CALIFORNIA
R. Yaqui
Rio Sonora
Rio Conchos
Rio Yaqui
Rio Mayo
R. Del Fuerte
SINALOA
Culiacan
Rio Culiacan
32
29
26
23
Longitude

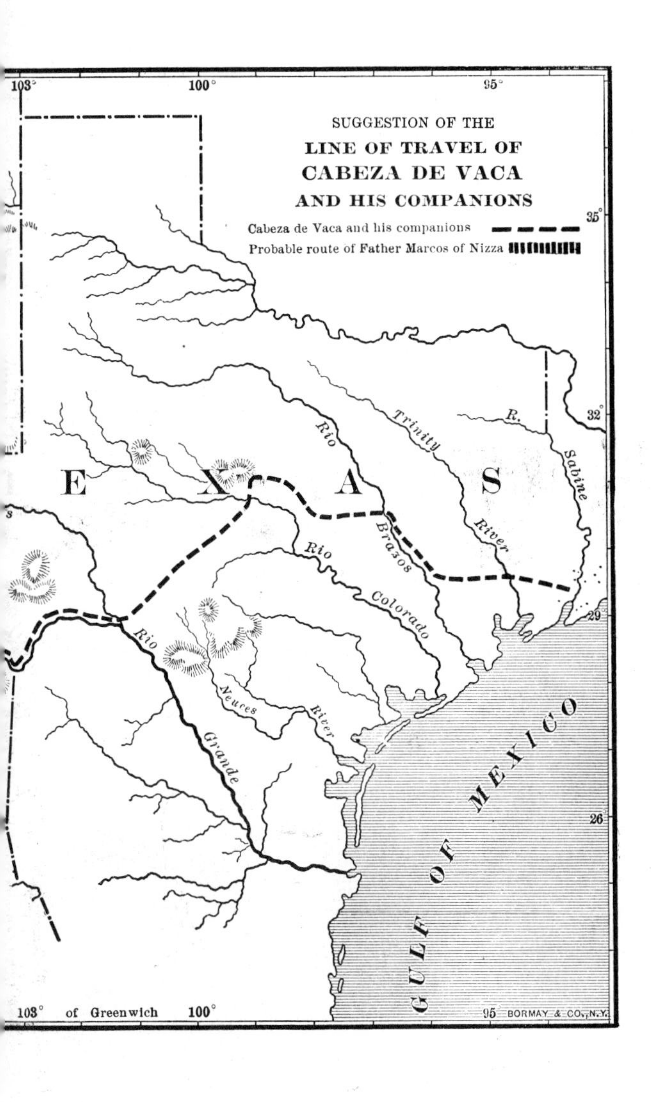
SUGGESTION OF THE
LINE OF TRAVEL OF
CABEZA DE VACA
AND HIS COMPANIONS
Cabeza de Vaca and his companions
Probable route of Father Marcos of Nizza
103°
100°
95°
35°
32°
29°
26°
E
X
A
S
Rio
Trinity
R.
Sabine
River
Brazos
Rio
Colorado
Rio
Neuces
River
Grande
GULF OF MEXICO
103° of Greenwich
100°
95
BORMAY & CO., N.Y.

in 1907 in the *Original Narratives of Early American History* in the volume *Spanish Explorers in the Southern United States, 1528-1543*, Hodge and Lewis, eds., (New York, Charles Scribner's Sons).

In an effort to produce a more precise translation, Fanny Bandelier set to work using the 1542 Zamora original. With the assistance of an introduction and notes by her prominent husband, Adolph F. Bandelier, the result was a work that has stood as the standard translation since 1905. In that year the book appeared as a volume of The Trail Maker series published by A. S. Barnes and Co. of New York. An identical edition was presented as a volume of the American Explorers series published in 1922 by the Allerton Book Co., New York.

Subsequent to the Bandelier editions several books have been written in English on Núñez Cabeza de Vaca. Most prominent have been Morris Bishop, *The Odyssey of Cabeza de Vaca* (New York, 1933), and Cleve Hallenbeck, *Alvar Núñez Cabeza de Vaca: The Journey and Route of the First European to cross the Continent of North America, 1534-1536* (Glendale, California, 1940). The former is biographical, while the latter is preoccupied with the route taken in these historic wanderings. Other historians have also been much concerned with the itinerary of the West's great early pedestrian. All have acknowledged a debt to Fanny Bandelier and her English language translation of Cabeza de Vaca's early descriptions. This, the best translation, has stood the test of time and has been chosen for reproduction as a Rio Grande Classic, which it is in a very real sense.

Donald C. Cutter
Professor of Southwestern History
University of New Mexico

Albuquerque, 1964

ABOUT THE AUTHOR OF THIS INTRODUCTION

Dr. Donald C. Cutter is presently Professor of Southwestern History at the University of New Mexico in Albuquerque. He was born in Chico, Calif., on Jan. 9, 1922. He took his undergraduate and graduate degrees from the University of California, A.B. (1943), M.A. (1947), Ph.D. (1950). From 1950 to 1951, Dr. Cutter was an Instructor at San Diego State College; from 1951 to 1962 an Assistant Professor and Professor of History at the University of Southern California; since 1962 he has been associated with the faculty of the University of New Mexico.

He heads the New Mexico Historical Review board, and is a member of the editorial boards of ARIZONA AND THE WEST, JOURNAL OF THE WEST, THE AMERICAN WEST, and THE AMERICAS. He has produced an impressive list of distinguished publications:

MALASPINA IN CALIFORNIA (1960)
THE DIARY OF ENSIGN GABRIEL MORAGA'S EXPEDITION OF DISCOVERY IN THE SACRAMENTO VALLEY, 1808 (1957)
TADEO HAENKE Y EL FINAL DE UNA VIEJA POLEMICA (in press, Buenos Aires)

He has contributed historical articles to:

ENCYCLOPEDIA BRITTANICA
COLLIER'S ENCYCLOPEDIA
HISPANIC AMERICAN HISTORICAL REVIEW
CALIFORNIA HISTORICAL SOCIETY QUARTERLY
REVISTA DE INDIAS
REVISTA DE HISTORIA MILITAR
PACIFIC NORTHWEST QUARTERLY
QUARTERLY OF THE HISTORICAL SOCIETY OF SOUTHERN CALIFORNIA
(and others)

Dr. Cutter has been a Fellow in Pacific Coast History, of the Native Sons of the Golden West; a Research Training Fellow in the Social Science Research Council; a Del Amo Foundation Fellow in Spain; A Faculty Research Fellow for the Social Science Research Council and a Fulbright Research Fellow in Spain.

The Rio Grande Press is most grateful to Dr. Cutter for his fine introduction to our reprint edition of THE JOURNEY OF ALVAR NUNEZ CABEZA DE VACA. We are honored and pleased that he was able to take the time from a very busy schedule to prepare this material, and we consider it a privilege to publish his words.

ROBERT B. McCOY, President
THE RIO GRANDE PRESS, INC.

October, 1964

THE JOURNEY OF

ALVAR NUNEZ CABEZA DE VACA

Lithographed By McKnight and McKnight Publishing
Bloomington, Illinois

Bound By Stappenbeck Bookbindery, Inc.
Bloomington, Illinois

THE JOURNEY OF ALVAR NUÑEZ CABEZA de VACA

AND HIS COMPANIONS FROM FLORIDA
TO THE PACIFIC
1528-1536

TRANSLATED FROM
HIS OWN NARRATIVE
By FANNY BANDELIER

TOGETHER WITH THE REPORT OF FATHER
MARCOS OF NIZZA AND A LETTER FROM
THE VICEROY MENDOZA

EDITED WITH AN INTRODUCTION BY
AD. F. BANDELIER

With Map

NEW YORK
A. S. BARNES & COMPANY
1905

¶ La relacion que dio Aluar nu-
ñez cabeça de vaca de lo acaescido enlas Indias
enla armada donde yua por gouernador Pã
philo de narbaez desde el año de veynte
y siete hasta el año de treynta y seys
que boluio a Seuilla con tres
de su compañia.:.

TITLE PAGE OF EDITION OF 1542.
Reduced fac-simile from the original in the Lenox
Branch of N. Y. Public Library.

INTRODUCTION

THIS volume offers the original narrative of the first white man to cross North America. The remarkable journey of Alvar Nuñez Cabeza de Vaca, Andrés Dorantes, Alonso del Castillo Maldonado, and the Moor Estévanico, from Florida to Northwestern Mexico (Sonora and Sinaloa), near the Pacific coast, antedates the expeditions of Coronado and De Soto, whose histories have already been published in *The Trail-Makers.* Nevertheless, it is proper to publish his narrative later. Compared with either of them, the journey of Cabeza de Vaca and his companions is an episode, important, but an incident brought about by a disastrous failure. This history describes the only — and comparatively meagre—results of the expedition undertaken by Pámfilo de Narvaez in 1527, and an outcome which had nothing more to do with Narvaez and his ill-conducted scheme.

Yet it is certain that the appearance of Cabeza de Vaca and his fellow-sufferers at Culiacan, and their statements, directed the attention of the Spanish authorities at the young city of Mexico to the North more than the reports about the Seven Cities and the raids which Nuño de Guzman had made in that direction. Nevertheless, the importance of the story of Cabeza de Vaca must not be overestimated. A perusal of the narrative shows that the forlorn wanderers were *not*—as it has long been admitted—the "discoverers of New Mexico." They never saw, nor do they claim to have seen, any of the so-called "Pueblos." They only *heard* of them, in a more or less confused manner. On the other hand, more precise than their information on this point is what they said about the plains, their Indians; and it seems above all doubt that the first knowledge of the American Bison, or Buffalo, is due to their descriptions.

On the minds of the Spanish occupants of Mexico, especially on what may be called the floating population (proportionately large at the time, as everywhere in newly occupied countries), the impression of the feat performed by the travellers and the tale of their unequalled sufferings produced a much greater effect than on the authorities. The people saw in their reports an outline for a possible advance into the unknown beyond. The picture of the country traversed was, in the main, not enticing, but the allusion to permanent settlements beyond the unprepossessing plains was looked upon as full of promise. The outcome was a moderate "excitement" among the adventurous and the idle, and this excitement was ably taken advantage of by the Viceroy of New Spain, Don Antonio de Mendoza.

This high functionary, as sagacious as he was cautious, regarded the real merits of Cabeza de Vaca (who is the representative figure in the whole episode) with reserve. On February 11th (old style), 1537, he wrote to the Empress recommending Cabeza de Vaca and Dorantes (the letter mentions Dorantes, but it was Castillo who went to Spain with Cabeza de Vaca) to the benevolence of the monarch, in consideration of "what they have done in it [this country] and suffered, and their disposition to continue there and here, wherever they may be sent." He does not seem to attach more than a modest importance to the practical results of their adventures. In that same letter he states that the wanderers had already made a report to him on their journey, which report he had sent to the Empress previously. It cannot be the one contained in Oviedo's *Historia General y Natural de Indias* (Edition of 1850, Vol. III, Lib. XXXV), since the latter was directed to the Audiencia of Santo Domingo. There is a fragment of a Relacion attributed to Cabeza de Vaca alone, without date, in Vol. XIV of the *Documentos Inéditos de Indias.* It reads like a *résumé,* or condensation, of the narrative presented in this volume. This fragment terminates abruptly at the time when a meeting of Cabeza de Vaca and Dorantes was being prepared. It is entitled, *"Relacion de Cabeza de Vaca, tesorero que fué en la conquista,"* and preceded by a truncated copy of the directions which the King issued to Cabeza de Vaca as "Factor" of the expedition. Whether this document (noticed in the *Index* under a very misleading title) is perhaps the first report mentioned in the letter of Mendoza from February, 1537, I am unable to decide thus far, but there are some indications favoring the supposition.

The influence which the return and reports of Cabeza de Vaca and companions may have had upon the subsequent enterprise of Hernando de Soto was, if any, but slight. The contract made with the latter by the Crown on April 20, 1537 (*Documentos de Indias,* Vol. XXII, pp. 534 to 546: *Capitulacion que se tomó con Hernando de Soto, para conquistar y poblar desde el Rio de las Palmas hasta la Florida*) does not permit any conclusion on this point. The first report of the outcasts had probably reached Spain before that time, but on August 15, of the same year, Cabeza de Vaca was still at Lisbon. The statements of other survivors of the expedition of Narvaez (mentioned at the close of our narrative as having been met by Cabeza de Vaca in Mexico and in Spain) cannot have been very encouraging to a fresh attempt at penetrating Florida.

Still, Soto tried to enlist the services of Cabeza de Vaca, but failed.

Of the biography of Cabeza de Vaca only such portions are well known as relate to his career in America. It is also known that he was born in Jeréz de la Frontera, in Spain, and hence was an Andalusian. His father—according to Oviedo—was Francisco de Vera, son of the Spanish Conqueror of the Canaries, Pedro de Vera. His mother was Teresa Cabeza de Vaca, a native of Jeréz. Why he assumed the name of his mother in place of his paternal appellative I am unable to state. The family of Cabeza de Vaca bore, originally, the name Alhaja. They were simple peasants until after the battle of Las Navas de Tolosa, on July 11, 1212, which the Kings of Castile, Aragon and Navarra gained over the Moors. A few days before the battle, a shepherd by the name of Alhaja offered to show the Christian forces a path by which they might circumvent the mountain-passes held by the Moors in strong force. To indicate it, he placed at the entrance of the defile the skull of a cow. In recompense for this eminent service, Martin Alhaja, until then a humble shepherd, was ennobled, and he changed his name into that of Cabeza de Vaca (head of a cow, literally) in memory of the origin of his improved social condition. Several of his descendants held comparatively high positions, among them Don Pero Fernandez Cabeza de Vaca, elected grand master of the order of Knights of St. James in 1383.

The career of Alvar Nuñez Cabeza de Vaca in America was particularly unfortunate. After the disastrous termination of Narvaez's expedition and his (almost miraculous) return to Spain, he obtained as a reward for his sufferings the position of Governor of the settlements on the La Plata river, vacant since the death of Pedro de Mendoza. Reaching his post in 1541, he soon became the object of sinister intrigues on the part of his subordinates. The animosity against him broke out, in 1543, in open revolt. He was seized and sent to Spain as a prisoner. His (mild) captivity there lasted eight years. It is asserted that he lived in Sevilla to an advanced age, and occupied, up to his demise (the date of which I have not yet been able to find), an honorable and fairly lucrative position.

Concerning the conduct of Cabeza de Vaca as Governor on the La Plata, or Paraná, the opinions of eye-witnesses are divided. Some speak in his favor; others, like the German Ulrich (or Huldreich) Schmiedel, of Straubing, accused him of haughty demeanor towards his men and cruelty. Oviedo, who knew him personally and conversed with him on the matter, is non-committal. It seems likely that Cabeza de Vaca was an honest and well-intentioned man, and he may have been a good subaltern but unfit for superior command. Hence he proved a failure as soon as raised to a position above the scope of his abilities.

Of the three companions of Cabeza de Vaca little is known. Andrés Dorantes, who had been a captain with Narvaez, was the son of Pablo Dorantes, a native of Gibraléon, Castilla. Maldonado was from Salamanca, and the son of Doctor Castillo and Aldonza Maldonado. He is said to have remained in Spain, whereas Dorantes stayed in Mexico, and entered, in 1538, into an agreement with the Viceroy for a journey of exploration to the north or Sinaloa. It was never carried out. Lastly the "negro," Estévanico was an Arab Moor, from the town of Azamor, on the Atlantic coast of Morocco. It is therefore not unlikely that he was not a negro proper, but from one or the other of the tribes of the desert. His subsequent fate is well known. As guide and advance scout of Father Marcos, of Nizza, he became the victim of his own imprudence, or lack of understanding of the differences in customs and beliefs between Indian tribes far distant from each other.

It is well known that Cabeza de Vaca wrote two principal works, both of which were published at Valladolid in 1555 by Francisco Fernandez de Córdova. The first one of these two books is a second issue of the one translated here. The other gives an account of his vicissitudes in Paraguay and what is now the Argentine Republic, and bears the title of *Comentarios de Alvar Nuñez Cabeza de Vaca, Adelantado y Gob-*

ernador del Rio de la Plata. The print from 1555 is the earliest known of the *Comentarios.* Of the *Naufragios* here translated an earlier issue has been found. Only two copies of it are known: One, which is perfect, is at the Lenox branch of the Public Library of New York; the other, somewhat damaged, at the British Museum. This oldest print of the *Naufragios* is from 1542 and was published at Zamora. Its text has been followed exclusively in this translation. The (reduced) photographic reproductions of the title-pages of both editions and of the kolophon of the first edition give an idea of the appearance of both of these books, the extreme rarity of which makes it difficult for the general reader to see them. Both are small quartos. The 1542 edition has no headings for chapters, and this has been followed here.

Oviedo, who gives the text in full of the Letter handed to the Audiencia of Santo Domingo by Cabeza de Vaca and Castillo when they touched that port on their return to Spain, in 1537, has used the 1542 print for comparison with that letter. The second edition appeared two years before his death (which occurred in 1557), but it is manifest that he did not use it.

Comparing the Letter to the Audiencia with the book of Cabeza de Vaca, Oviedo inclines in favor of the former. He remarks: "But in a certain way I hold the report of the three to be good and more clear than the other one, which a single man made and has had printed," &c. But Cabeza de Vaca was one of the three who framed the Letter to the Audiencia, and this document is merely a more concise narration than his book, and does not, on important points, conflict with it. The latter was written in Spain, when the author had leisure to recollect and to write. In a foot-note I have alluded to the statement, made in the book, about little bags filled with silver, which, Oviedo says, contained only mica. This, however, he distinctly attributes to a *misprint,* not to a *misstatement* by the author. On the whole, the difference between the two documents is so slight that there has been no occasion to publish the Letter to the Audiencia also.

Oviedo mentions Andrés Dorantes among the signers of the Letter, which was, as he states, sent to the Audiencia at Santo Domingo from Havana. Cabeza de Vaca affirms Dorantes remained at Vera Cruz, and thence went back to Mexico. This is fully established by the communications of the Viceroy, Mendoza, notwithstanding Herrera says he returned to Spain with his companions. The objection may be removed, however, by supposing, as is very likely, that the Letter was writen in Mexico, when the three were still together.

A very serious objection to the credibility of the three narratives, however, arises from the fact that all are based upon recollections only, and not upon journals or field-notes of any kind. It was, of course, impossible for the outcasts, shifted and shifting from tribe to tribe, to keep any written record of their trip. Many of their descriptions are not, therefore, expected to be fully accurate.

At the end of the eight years of constant misfortune and suffering, memory clings most to personal vicissitudes, and the narrative of these does not appear exaggerated.

The descriptions of the countries traversed, superficial as they must be, still leave some recognizable data, and so do the descriptions of plants and animals. It is acknowledged that through Cabeza de Vaca the first knowledge of the buffalo reached Europe, and his description of the hunchbacked cows, while very brief, is quite accurate.

Descriptions of customs and habits of Indian tribes or bands, especially of such as lived east of the Rio Grande, must of course be accepted with proper reserve. Still, many may yet prove to be of ethnologic value. The general picture of the condition of these tribes is very likely to be exact, while, on the other hand, many details are probably misstated, through having been misunderstood or superficially observed. It might be worth while to make a special study of these ethnographic data and compare them with whatever material of the kind has been placed on record by subsequent explorers and narrators.

In the statements regarding the "faith cures" which the travellers claim to have performed, and to which they attribute the success of their desperate attempt to cross the continent, there is truth as well as honest delusion. Indian medicine itself bases largely upon conceptions of the kind, and empirical hypnotism plays a part in the performances of their medicine-men. Cabeza de Vaca, unconsciously and by distinct methods, imitated the Indian Shamans and probably succeeded, in at least many cases, since the procedure was new and striking. That they attributed their success to the direct aid of divine power was in strict accordance with the spirit of the times and by no means to their discredit. On the contrary, there is a commendable modesty in their disclaimer of merits of their own. It should also not be forgotten that men in their exceptional situation, without reasonable hope of salvation, relentlessly persecuted by misfortune and the worst hardships for many years, have their imagination finally raised to the higest pitch, and exaggerations and misconceptions become therefore excusable. There is no doubt that they sincerely believed their own statements. Not only the times must be taken into account when judgment is passed, but also the violent strain under which they labored for such a long period.

In regard to the route followed by the outcasts, there are but very few ascertained points. Opinions vary so much that I shall not attempt to trace the course of their wanderings except by referring to the sketch-map appended. The route traced is a mere suggestion of possible approximations, as stated on it. It will certainly be modified by the results of investigations in the countries themselves, which I have not been and am not able to carry on myself. It seems, however, that the overland journey of the four began at some point west of the Mississippi, and that they successively traversed the State of Texas and the northern part of the Mexican Republic into central Sonora. It is not likely they touched New Mexico, and they certainly never saw the New Mexican pueblos, but heard of them in Sonora. Cabeza de Vaca therefore but confirmed the few vague notions extant at his time about the sedentary Indians of New Mexico, but was not the real discoverer of that country.

INTRODUCTION

The bibliography of the book of Cabeza de Vaca is soon told. In addition to the two issues often mentioned—the *Editio Princeps* from 1542, and the second of 1555—there are two more Spanish publications of it known. The earliest is in Volume II of the Collection by Andrés Gonzales Bárcia, *Historiades primitivos de Indias,* 1749. Its title is: *Naufragios y relacion de la Jornada que hizo á la Florida, con Pánfilo de Narvaez.*

The other is found in Volume II of the *Historiadores primitivos de Indias, by Enrique de Vedia.* The title of this (the text of which was taken from the Edition of 1555) reads: *Naufragios de Alvar Nuñez Cabeza de Vaca y Relacion de la Jornada que hizo á la Florida con el Adelantado Pánfilo de Narvaez.* It is well known that the two volumes of Vedia's reprints of older narratives and histories touching upon America form a part of the voluminous collection entitled, *Bibliotéca de Autores Españoles,* published at Madrid, and that the two volumes of Vedia were printed in 1852.

An Italian version, under the title of *Relation che fece Alvaro Nunez detto Capo di*

Vacca, di quello ch' intervenne nell India all' armata, della qual era gouernatore Pamphilo Naruaez, dell anno 1527 fino all 1536, che ritorno in Sibilla con tu soli suoi compagni, is contained in Volume II of the celebrated collection of travels and voyages by Gian Battista Ramusio, *Delle Navigatione è Viaggi,* 1556, Venice.

Of English translations there have appeared thus far three: In Samuel Purchas: *His Pilgrimage,* London, 1625-1626, Volume IX: *Relation of the fleet in India, whereof Pamphilus Naruaez was gouernor. The Narrative of Alva Nuñez Cabeza de Vaca,* translated by Buckingham Smith, Washington, 1851. This translation is justly prized. A second edition of it appeared at New York in 1871, edited by the late John Gilmary Shea. Finally there is a paraphrase of the book in *Tales of Old Travels, Narrated by H. Kingsley,* London, 1869.

In the French language there is the well-known translation by H. Ternaux Compans in the first series of his collection: *Voyages, Relations et Mémoires originaux pour servir à l'Histoire de la Découverte de l'Amérique.*

Date of publication, 1837. Title: *Relation Vaca, Adelantade et Gouverneur du Rio de la Plata.*

A word yet touching the translation here given. The narrative of Cabeza de Vaca is very difficult to translate for the reason, that the criticism by Oviedo about its lack of clearness is too well founded. Many parts of chapters and also whole chapters are so confused that it is impossible to follow the original more than remotely, and paraphrasing had to be resorted to. Even then, in several instances, the meaning remains possibly somewhat obscure. It is as if the author, in consequence of long isolation and constant intercourse with people of another speech, had lost touch with his native tongue. There is less of this in his later work, the *Comentarios,* written after a number of years of uninterrupted intercourse with his countrymen.

AD. F. BANDELIER.

NEW YORK CITY, March 28, 1905.

¶ La relacion y comentarios del gouerna dor Aluar nuñez cabeça de vaca, de lo acaescido en las dos jornadas que hizo a las Indias.

Con priuilegio.

¶ Esta tassada por los señores del consejo en Ochēta y cinco mrs.

TITLE PAGE OF EDITION OF 1555.
Reduced from original in Lenox Branch of N. Y. Public Library.

The Journey of Alvar Nunez Cabeza De Vaca

ON the 27th day of the month of June, 1527,[1] the Governor Panfilo de Narvaez departed from the port of San Lucar de Barrameda, with authority and orders from Your Majesty to conquer and govern the provinces that extend from the river of the Palms to the Cape of the Florida, these provinces being on the main land. The fleet he took along consisted of five vessels, in which went about 600 men. The officials he had with him (since they must be mentioned) were those here named: Cabeza de Vaca, treasurer and alguacil mayor; Alonso Enriquez, purser; Alonso de Solis, factor of Your Majesty and inspector. A friar of the order of Saint Francis, called Fray Juan Gutierrez,[2] went as commissary,

[1]All the dates are old style, of course.

[2]The edition of 1555 and subsequent publications have Fray Juan Suarez, which the first edition from 1542 also has, as will be seen subsequently, so that the name of this Commissary of the Franciscans must have been Suarez, or (as it is also written) Xuarez.

with four other monks of the order. We arrived at the Island of Santo Domingo, where we remained nearly forty-five days, supplying ourselves with necessary things, especially horses. Here more than 140 men of our army forsook us, who wished to remain, on account of the proposals and promises made them by the people of the country. From there we started and arrived at Santiago (a port in the Island of Cuba) where, in the few days that we remained the Governor supplied himself again with people, arms and horses. It happened there that a gentleman called Vasco Porcallo, a resident of la Trinidad (which is on the same island), offered to give the Governor certain stores he had at a distance of 100 leagues from the said harbor of Santiago.

The Governor, with the whole fleet, sailed for that place, but midways, at a port named Cape Santa Cruz, he thought best to stop and send a single vessel to load and bring these stores. Therefore he ordered a certain Captain Pantoja to go thither with his craft and directed me to accompany him for the sake of control, while he remained with four ships, having purchased one on the Island of Santo Domingo. Arrived at the port of Trinidad with these two vessels, Captain Pantoja went with Vasco Porcallo to the town (which is one league from there) in order to take possession of the supplies. I remained on board with the pilots, who told us that we should leave as soon as possible, since the harbor was very unsafe and many vessels had been lost in it. Now, since what happened to us there was very remarkable, it appeared to me not unsuitable, for the aims and ends of this, my narrative, to tell it here.

The next morning the weather looked ominous. It began to rain, and the sea roughened so that, although I allowed the men to land, when they saw the weather and that the town was one league away, many came back to the ship so as not to be out in the wet and cold. At the same time there came a canoe from the town conveying a letter from a person residing there, begging me to come, and they would give me the stores and whatever else might be necessary. But I excused myself, stating that I could not leave the ships.

At noon the canoe came again with another letter, repeating the request with much insistency, and there was also a horse for me to go on. I gave the same reply as the first time, saying that I could not leave the vessels. But the pilots and the people begged me so much to leave and hasten the transportation of the stores to the ships, in order to be able to sail soon, from a place where they were in great fear the ships would be lost in case they had to remain long. So I determined upon going, although before I went I left the pilots well instructed and with orders in case the south wind (which often wrecked the shipping) should rise, and they found themselves in great danger, to run the vessels ashore, when men and horses might be saved. So I left, wishing for some of them to accompany me, but they refused, alleging the hard rain, the cold and that the town was far away.

On the next day, which was Sunday, they promised to come, God helping, to hear mass. One hour after my departure the sea became very rough and the north wind blew so fiercely that neither did the boats dare to land, nor could they beach the vessels, since the wind was blowing from the shore. They spent that day and Sunday greatly distressed by two contrary storms and much rain, until nightfall. Then the rain and storm increased in violence at the village, as well as on the sea, and all the houses and the churches fell down, and we had to go about, seven or eight men locking arms at a time, to prevent the wind from carrying us off, and under the trees it was not less dangerous than among the houses, for as they also were blown down we were in danger of being killed beneath them. In this tempest and peril we wandered about all night, without finding any part or place where we might feel safe for half an hour.

In this plight we heard, all night long and especially after midnight, a great uproar, the sound of many voices, the tinkling of little bells, also flutes and tambourines and other instruments, the most of which noise lasted until morning, when the storm ceased.

Never has such a fearful thing been witnessed in those parts. I took testimony concerning it, and sent it, certified, to Your Majesty. On Monday morning we went down to the harbor, but did not find the vessels. We saw the buoys in the water, and from this knew that the ships were lost. So we followed the shore, looking for wreckage, and not finding any turned into the forest. Walking through it we saw, a fourth of a league from water, the little boat of one of the vessels on the top of trees, and ten leagues further, on the coast, were two men of my crew and certain covers of boxes. The bodies were so disfigured by striking against the rocks as to be unrecognizable. There were also found a cape and a tattered quilt, nothing else. Sixty people and twenty horses perished on the ships. Those who went on land the day we arrived, some thirty men, were all who survived of the crews of both vessels.

We remained thus for several days in great need and distress, for the food and stores at the village had been ruined also, as well as some cattle. The country was pitiable to look at. The trees had fallen and the woods were blighted, and there was neither foliage nor grass. In this condition we were until the 5th day of the month of November, when the Governor, with his four vessels, arrived. They also had weathered a great storm and had escaped by betaking themselves to a safe place in time. The people on board of the ships and those he found were so terrified by what had happened that they were afraid to set to sea again in winter and begged the Governor to remain there for that season, and he, seeing their good will and that of the inhabitants, wintered at that place. He put into my charge the vessels and their crews, and I was to go with them to the port of Xagua, twelve leagues distant, where I remained until the 20th day of February.

AT that time the Governor came with a brig he had bought at Trinidad, and with him a pilot called Miruelo. That man he had taken because he said he knew the way and had been on the river of the Palms and was a very good pilot for the whole northern coast. The Governor left, on the coast of Habana, another vessel that he had bought there, on which there remained, as captain, Alvaro de Cerda, with forty people and twelve horsemen. Two days after the Governor arrived he went aboard. The people he took along were 400 men and eighty horses, on four vessels and one brigantine. The pilot we had taken ran the vessels aground on the sands called "of Canarreo," so that the next day we were stranded and remained stranded for fifteen days, the keels often touching bottom. Then a storm from the south drove so much water on the shoals that we could get off, though not without much danger.

Departing from there and arrived at Guaniguanico, another tempest came up in which we nearly perished. At Cape Corrientes we had another, which lasted three days. Afterward we doubled the Cape of Sant Anton and sailed with contrary winds as far as twelve leagues off Habana, and when, on the following day, we attempted to enter, a southerly storm drove us away, so that we crossed to the coast of Florida, sighting land on Tuesday, the 12th day of the month of April.[3] We coasted the way of Florida, and on Holy Thursday cast anchor at the mouth of a bay, at the head of which we saw certain houses and habitations of Indians.

ON that same day the clerk, Alonso Enriquez, left and went to an island in the bay and called the Indians, who came and were with him a good while, and by way of exchange they gave him fish and some venison. The day following (which was Good Friday) the Governor disembarked, with as many men as his little boats would hold, and as we arrived at the huts or houses of the Indians we had seen, we found them abandoned and deserted, the

[3]Same date in Oviedo (*Historia general y natural de Indias,* Vol. III, p. 582. But the details of the stay on the coast and in the ports of Cuba are only found in Cabeza de Vaca's book, and in his *Relacion* (*Documentos de Indias,* Vol. XIV, p. 289), where he mentions two tempests: the great hurricane and one that nearly wrecked them near Cape Corrientes. That *Relacion* seems like an abridgement of the *Naufragios.*

people having left that same night in their canoes. One of those houses was so large that it could hold more than 300 people. The others were smaller, and we found a golden rattle among the nets. The next day the Governor hoisted flags in behalf of Your Majesty and took possession of the country in Your Royal name, exhibited his credentials, and was acknowledged as Governor according to Your Majesty's commands. We likewise presented our titles to him, and he complied as they required. He then ordered the remainder of the men to disembark, also the forty-two horses left (the others having perished on account of the great storms and the long time they had been on sea), and these few that remained were so thin and weak that they could be of little use for the time. The next day the Indians of that village came, and, although they spoke to us, as we had no interpreters we did not understand them; but they made many gestures and threats, and it seemed as if they beckoned to us to leave the country. Afterward, without offering any molestation, they went away.

AFTER another day the Governor resolved to penetrate inland to explore the country and see what it contained. We went with him—the commissary, the inspector and myself, with forty men, among them six horsemen, who seemed likely to be of but little use. We took the direction of the north, and at the hour of vespers reached a very large bay, which appeared to sweep far inland. After remaining there that night and the next day, we returned to the place where the vessels and the men were. The Governor ordered the brigantine to coast towards Florida in search of the port which Miruelo, the pilot, had said he knew, but he had missed it and did not know where we were, nor where the port was. So word was sent to the brigantine, in case it were not found to cross over to Habana in quest of the vessel of Alvaro de la Cerda, and, after taking in some supplies, to come after us again.

After the brigantine left we again penetrated inland, the same persons as before, with some more men. We followed the ihore of the bay, and, after a march of four eagues, captured four Indians, to whom we ihowed maize in order to find out if they cnew it, for until then we had seen no trace of it. They told us that they would take us o a place where there was maize and they ed us to their village, at the end of the bay iearby, and there they showed us some that vas not yet fit to be gathered. There we ound many boxes for merchandize from Castilla. In every one of them was a corpse overed with painted deer hides. The comnissary thought this to be some idolatrous ractice, so he burnt the boxes with the orpses. We also found pieces of linen and loth, and feather head dresses that seemed o be from New Spain, and samples of gold.

We inquired of the Indians (by signs) vhence they had obtained these things and hey gave us to understand that, very far rom there, was a province called Apalachen n which there was much gold.[4] They also

[4]There is a discrepancy here between the statement of Cabeza de Vaca and the Letter to the udiencia. The latter says (*Historia, &c.*, III, 583): "And there they found some large boxes om Castilla, and in each of them a dead man, nd the corpses covered with painted hides. It

signified to us that in that province we would find everything we held in esteem. They said that in Apalachen there was plenty.

So, taking them as guides, we started, and after walking ten or twelve leagues, came to another village of fifteen houses, where there was a large cultivated patch of corn

appeared to the Commissary and friars that these were idolatries, so the Governor had them burnt. There were also found pieces of shoes and canvas (*lienzo*), of cloth and some iron, and inquiring of the Indians they told us by signs that they had found it in a vessel that had been lost on this coast and in that bay."

The text of Oviedo discriminates between the origin of these objects and that of the gold, which it says the Indians declared that there was none in the country, but at Apalache, very far away. The first edition always has either Apalachen or Palachen. Oviedo (p. 615) justly blames the friars for having burnt the bodies: "Since the boxes and other indications might have led them to think that they were the bodies of Christians, and so it is stated in the second relation, that they learned from Indians that these dead people had been Christians." The *Relacion* (p. 270) mentions briefly the bodies, and also states that gold was found in the province of Apalache.

The shipwreck mentioned may allude to the loss, in 1526, of one of the two vessels in which Lucas Vazquez de Ayllon made his unlucky voyage to Chicora. This vessel was lost at the mouth of the "Rio Jordon" Herrera (*Historia general, &c.*, 1726, Vol. II, p. 242, Decada III, Lib. VII, Cap. XIII). Still, this is conjectural and requires special investigation, which does not enter into the scope of these notes.

nearly ready for harvest, and also some that was already ripe. After staying there two days, we returned to the place where we had left the purser, the men and the vessels, and told the purser and pilots what we saw and the news the Indians had given us.

The next day, which was the 1st of May, the Governor took aside the commissary, the purser, the inspector, myself, a sailor called Bartolomé Fernandez and a notary by the name of Jerónimo de Albaniz, and told us that he had in mind to penetrate inland, while the vessels should follow the coast as far as the harbor; since the pilots said and believed that, if they went in the direction of the Palms they would reach it soon. On this he asked us to give our opinions.

I replied that it seemed to me in no manner advisable to forsake the ships until they were in a safe port, held and occupied by us. I told him to consider that the pilots were at a loss, disagreeing among themselves, undecided as to what course to pursue. Moreover, the horses would not be with us in case we needed them, and, furthermore, we had no interpreter to make ourselves understood by the natives; hence we could have no parley with them. Neither did we know what to expect from the land we were entering, having no knowledge of what it was, what it might contain and by what kind of people it was inhabited, nor in what part of it we were; finally, that we had not the supplies required for penetrating into an unknown country, for of the stores left in the ships not more than one pound of biscuit and one of bacon could be given as rations to each man for the journey, so that, in my opinion, we should re-embark and sail in quest of a land and harbor better adapted to settlement, since the country which we had seen was the most deserted and the poorest ever found in those parts.

The commissary was of the contrary opinion saying, that we should not embark, but follow the coast in search of a harbor, as the pilots asserted that the way to Pánuco was not more than ten or fifteen leagues distant and that by following along the coast it was impossible to miss it, since the coast bent inland for twelve leagues. The first ones who came there should wait for the others. As to embarking, he said it would be to tempt God, after all the vicissitudes of storms, losses of men and vessels and hardships we had suffered since leaving Spain, and until we came to that place. So his advice would be to move along the coast as far as the harbor, while the vessels with the other men would follow to the same port.

To all the others this seemed to be the best, except to the notary, who said that before leaving the ships they should be put into a harbor well known, safe and in a settled country, after which we might go inland and do as we liked.

The Governor clung to his own idea and to the suggestions of the others.

Seeing his determination, I required him, on the part of Your Majesty, not to forsake the vessels until they were in a secure port, and I asked the notary present to testify to what I said. The Governor replied that he approved the opinion of the other officials and of the commissary; that I had no authority for making such demands, and he asked the notary to give him a certified statement as to how, there not being in the country the means for supporting a settlement, nor any harbor for the ships, he broke up the village he had founded, and went in search of the port and of a better land. So he forthwith ordered the people who were to go with him to get ready, providing themselves with what was necessary for the journey. After this he turned to me, and told me in the presence of all who were there that, since I so much opposed the expedition into the interior and was afraid of it, I should take charge of the vessels and men remaining, and, in case I reached the port before him, I should settle there. This I declined.

After the meeting was over he, on that same evening, saying that it seemed to him as if he could not trust anybody, sent me word that he begged me to take charge of that part of the expedition, and as, in spite of his insistency, I declined, he asked for the reasons of my refusal, I then told him that I refused to accept, because I felt sure he would never see the ships again, or be seen by their crews any more; that, seeing how utterly unprepared he was for moving inland, I preferred to share the risk with him and his people, and suffer what they would have to suffer, rather than take charge of the vessels and thus give occasion for saying that I opposed the journey and remained out of fear, which would place my honor in jeopardy. So that I would much rather expose of my life than, under these circumstances, my good name.

Seeing that he could not change my determination, he had others approach me about it with entreaties. But I gave the same answer to them as to him, and he finally provided for his lieutenant to take command of the vessels, an alcalde named Caravallo.

ON Saturday, the 1st of May, the day on which all this had happened, he ordered that they should give to each one of those who had to go with him, two pounds of ship-biscuit and one-half pound of bacon, and thus we set out upon our journey inland. The number of people we took along was three hundred,[5] among them the commissary, Father Juan Xuarez, another friar called Father Juan de Palos and three priests, the officers, and forty horsemen. We marched for fifteen days, living on the supplies we had taken with us, without finding anything else to eat but palmettos like those of Andalusia. In all this time we did not meet a soul, nor did we see a house or village, and finally reached a river, which we crossed with much trouble, by swimming and on rafts. It took us a day to ford the river on account of the swiftness of its current. When we got across, there came towards us some two hundred Indians, more or less; the Governor went to meet them, and after he talked to them by signs they acted in such a manner that we were obliged to set upon them and seize five or six, who took us to their houses, about half a league from there, where we found a large quantity of corn ready for harvest. We gave infinite thanks to our Lord for having help-

[5]Oviedo (*Historia*, III, p. 584) says, following the Letter to the Audiencia, 260 foot and forty horse. The *Relacion* (p. 270) three hundred men *and* forty men on horseback (*"trescientos hombres y quarenta hombres de á caballo"*).

ed us in such great need, for, as we were not used to such exposures, we felt greatly exhausted, and were much weakened by hunger.

On the third day that we were at this place the purser, the inspector, the commissary and myself jointly begged the Governor to send out in search of a harbor, as the Indians told us the sea was not very far away. He forbade us to speak of it, saying it was at a great distance, and I being the one who most insisted, he bade me to go on a journey of discovery and search of a port, and said I should go on foot with forty people. So the next day I started with the Captain Alonso del Castillo and forty men of his company. At noon we reached sandy patches that seemed to extend far inland. For about one and a half leagues we walked, with the water up to the knee, and stepping on shells that cut our feet badly. All this gave us much trouble, until we reached the river which we had crossed first, and which emptied through the same inlet, and then, as we were too ill-provided for crossing it, we turned back to camp and told the Governor what we had found and how it was necessary to ford the river again at our first crossing in order to explore the inlet thoroughly and find out if there was a harbor.

The next day he sent a captain called Valenzuela with sixty footmen and six horsemen to cross the river and follow its course to the sea in search of a port. After two days he came back, reporting that he had discovered the inlet, which was a shallow bay, with water to the knees, but it had there no harbor. He saw five or six canoes crossing from one side to the other, with Indians who wore many feather bushes.

Hearing this, we left the next day, always in quest of the province called Apalachen by the Indians, taking as guides those whom we had captured, and marched until the 17th of June without finding an Indian who would dare to wait for us. Finally there came to us a chief, whom an Indian carried on his shoulders. He wore a painted deerskin, and many people followed him, and he was preceded by many players on flutes made of reeds. He came to the place where the Governor was and stayed an hour. We gave him to understand by signs that our aim was to reach Apalachen, but from his gestures it seemed to us that he was an enemy of the Apalachen people and that he would go and help us against them. We gave him beads and little bells and other trinkets, while he presented the Governor with the hide he wore. Then he turned back and we followed him.

That night we reached a broad and deep river, the current of which was very strong and as we did not dare to cross it, we built a canoe out of rafts and were a whole day in getting across. If the Indians had wished to oppose us, they could have easily impeded our passage, for even with their help we had much trouble. One horseman, whose name was Juan Velazquez, a native of Cuéllar, not willing to wait, rode into the stream, and the strong current swept him from the horse and he took hold of the reins, and was drowned with the animal. The Indians of that chief (whose name was Dulchanchellin) discovered the horse and told us that we would find him lower down the stream. So they went after the man, and his death caused us much grief, since until then we had not lost anybody. The horse made a supper for many on that night. Beyond there, and on the following day, we reached the chief's village, whither he sent us corn.

That same night, as they went for water, an arrow was shot at one of the Christians, but God willed that he was not hurt. The day after we left this place, without any of the natives having appeared, because all had fled, but further on some Indians were seen who showed signs of hostility, and although we called them they would neither come back nor wait, but withdrew and followed in our rear. The Governor placed a few horsemen in ambush near the trail, who as they (the Indians) passed, surprised them and took three or four Indians, whom we kept as guides thereafter. These led us into a country difficult to traverse and strange to look at, for it had very great forests, the trees being wonderfully tall and so many of them fallen that they obstructed our way so that we had to make long detours and with great trouble.

Of the trees standing many were rent from top to bottom by thunderbolts, which strike very often in that country, where storms and tempests are always frequent.

With such efforts we travelled until the day after St. John's Day, when we came in sight of Apalachen, without having been noticed by the Indians of the land. We gave many thanks to God for being so near it, believing what we had been told about the country to be true, and that now our sufferings would come to an end after the long and weary march over bad trails. We had also suffered greatly from hunger, for, although we found corn occasionally, most of the time we marched seven or eight leagues without any. And many there were among us who besides suffering great fatigue and hunger, had their backs covered with wounds from the weight of the armor and other things they had to carry as occasion required. But to find ourselves at last where we wished to be and where we had been assured so much food and gold would be had, made us forget a great deal of our hardships and weariness.

ALVAR NUNEZ CABEZA DE VACA

ONCE in sight of Apalachen,[6] the Governor commanded me to enter the village with nine horsemen and fifty foot. So the inspector and I undertook this. Upon penetrating into the village we found only women and boys. The men were not there at the time, but soon, while we were walking about, they came and began to fight, shooting arrows at us. They killed the inspector's horse, but finally fled and left us. We found there plenty of ripe maize ready to be gathered and much dry corn already housed. We also found many deer skins and among them mantles made of thread and of poor quality, with which the women cover parts of their bodies. They had many vessels for grinding maize.[7] The village contained forty small and low

[6]This Indian village seems to have been situated west of the peninsula of Florida, not far from the coast. Without presuming to insist upon its location, I would only remark that it might have been on or near what is now the Apalachicola river. At least, the French map accompanying the *Historical Collections of Louisiana* (Part II, 185, 1850) has: "*Apalaches. Ici étaient ci-devant les Apalaches.*"

[7]The text says: "*Tenian muchos vasos para moler maiz.*" This seems to indicate mortars.

houses,[8] reared in sheltered places, out of fear of the great storms that continuously occur in the country. The buildings are of straw, and they are surrounded by dense timber, tall trees and numerous water-pools, where there were so many fallen trees and of such size as to greatly obstruct and impede circulation.

THE country between our landing place and the village and country of Apalachen is mostly level; the soil is sand and earth. All throughout it there are very large trees and open forests containing nut trees, laurels and others of the kind called resinous, cedar, juniper, water-oak, pines, oak and low palmetto, like those of Castilla.[9] Everywhere there are many

[8]I use the word "house" here, but I shall hereafter prefer the term of "lodge." It is more in harmony with the character of the frail constructions which he describes. Later on, when Cabeza de Vaca alludes to more substantial structures, I shall again employ the term "house." In general, "*casa*" in Spanish means house, dwelling, home, abode, &c.

[9]The original has: "*Donde hay nogales y laureles y otros que se llaman liquid-ámbares, cedros sabinos y encinas y pinos y robles, palmitos bajos, de la manera de los de Castilla.*" *Luquid-ámbar* is the product of a species of the Mexican pine, besides being amber proper.

lagunes, large and small, some very difficult to cross, partly because they are so deep, partly because they are covered with fallen trees. Their bottom is sandy, and in the province of Apalachen the lagunes are much larger than those we found previously. There is much maize in this province and the houses are scattered all over the country as much as those of the Gelves. The animals we saw there were three kinds of deer, rabbits and hares, bears and lions and other wild beasts, among them one that carries its young in a pouch on its belly as long as the young are small, until they are able to look for their sustenance, and even then, when they are out after food and people come, the mother does not move until her little ones are in the pouch again. The country is very cold;[10] it has good pasture for cattle; there are birds of many kinds in large numbers: geese, ducks, wild ducks, muscovy ducks, Ibis, small white herons (Egrets), herons and partridges. We saw many falcons, marsh-hawks, sparrow-hawks, pigeon-

[10]It is somewhat puzzling to read this, since it was midsummer when Narvaez reached Apalachen.

hawks and many other birds.[11] Two hours after we arrived at Apalachen the Indians that had fled came back peaceably, begging us to give back to them their women and children, which we did.[12] The Governor, however, kept with him one of their caciques, at which they became so angry as to attack us the following day. They did it so swiftly and with so much audacity as to set fire to the lodges we occupied, but when we sallied forth they fled to the lagunes nearby, on account of which and of the big corn patches, we could not do them any harm beyond killing one Indian. The day after, Indians from a village on the other side came and attacked us in the same manner, escaping in the same way, with the loss of a single man.

We remained at this village for twenty-

[11]"*Hay aves de muchas maneras, ansares en gran cantidad, pasos, ánades, patos reales, dorales y garzotas y garzas, perdices; vimos muchos halcones, neblis, gavilanes, esmorejanes, y otras muchas aves.*" The "*dorales*" are ibis, the "*nebli*" corresponds to the marsh-hawk, and the nearest approach to the "*esmorejan*" might be the pigeon-hawk, perhaps. The "*garzota*" is the egret.

[12]To return the non-combatants to the Indians was not very wise, and shows that Narvaez and his officers had little knowledge of Indian nature.

five days, making three excursions during the time. We found the country very thinly inhabited and difficult to march through, owing to bad places, timber and lagunes. We inquired of the cacique whom we had retained and of the other Indians with us (who were neighbors and enemies of them) about the condition and settlements of the land, the quality of its people, about supplies and everything else. They answered, each one for himself, that Apalachen was the largest town of all; that further in less people were met with, who were very much poorer than those here, and that the country was thinly settled, the inhabitants greatly scattered, and also that further inland big lakes, dense forests, great deserts and wastes were met with.

Then we asked about the land to the south, its villages and resources. They said that in that direction and nine days' march towards the sea was a village called Aute,[13] where the Indians had plenty of corn and also beans and melons, and that, being so near

[13]On the map in Louisiana historical collections, already mentioned, *Aute*, is placed near the mouth of the Apalachicola river.

the sea, they obtained fish, and that those were their friends. Seeing how poor the country was, taking into account the unfavorable reports about its population and everything else, and that the Indians made constant war upon us, wounding men and horses whenever they went for water (which they could do from the lagunes where we could not reach them) by shooting arrows at us; that they had killed a chief of Tezcuco called Don Pedro, whom the commissary had taken along with him, we agreed to depart and go in search of the sea, and of the village of Aute, which they had mentioned. And so we left, arriving there five days after. The first day we travelled across lagunes and trails without seeing a single Indian.

On the second day, however, we reached a lake very difficult to cross, the water reaching to the chest, and there were a great many fallen trees. Once in the middle of it, a number of Indians assailed us from behind trees that concealed them from our sight, while others were on fallen trees, and they began to shower arrows upon us, so that many men and horses were wounded, and before we could get out of the lagune our guide was captured by them. After we had got out, they pressed us very hard, intending to cut us off, and it was useless to turn upon them, for they would hide in the lake and from there wound both men and horses.

So the Governor ordered the horsemen to dismount and attack them on foot. The pursuer dismounted also, and our people attacked them. Again they fled to a lagune, and we succeeded in holding the trail. In this fight some of our people were wounded, in spite of their good armor. There were men that day who swore they had seen two oak trees, each as thick as the calf of a leg, shot through and through by arrows, which is not surprising if we consider the force and dexterity with which they shoot. I myself saw an arrow that had penetrated the base of a poplar tree for half a foot in length. All the many Indians from Florida we saw were archers, and, being very tall and naked, at a distance they appear giants.

Those people are wonderfully built, very

gaunt and of great strength and agility. Their bows are as thick as an arm, from eleven to twelve spans long, shooting an arrow at 200 paces with unerring aim. From that crossing we went to another similar one, a league away, but while it was half a league in length it was also much more difficult. There we crossed without opposition, for the Indians, having spent all their arrows at the first place, had nothing wherewith they would dare attack us. The next day, while crossing a similar place, I saw the tracks of people who went ahead of us, and I notified the Governor, who was in the rear, so that, although the Indians turned upon us, as we were on our guard, they could do us no harm. Once on open ground they pursued us still. We attacked them twice, killing two, while they wounded me and two or three other Christians, and entered the forest again, where we could no longer injure them.

In this manner we marched for eight days, without meeting any more natives, until one league from the site to which I said we were going. There, as we were marching along, Indians crept up unseen and fell upon our rear. A boy belonging to a nobleman, called Avellaneda, who was in the rear guard, gave the alarm. Avellaneda turned back to assist, and the Indians hit him with an arrow on the edge of the cuirass, piercing his neck nearly through and through, so that he died on the spot, and we carried him to Aute. It took us nine days from Apalachen to the place where we stopped.[14] And then we found that all the people had left and the lodges were burnt. But there was plenty of maize, squash and beans, all nearly ripe and ready for harvest. We rested there for two days.

After this the Governor entreated me to go in search of the sea, as the Indians said it was so near by, and we had, on this march, already suspected its proximity from a great river to which we had given the name of the *Rio de la Magdalena*.[15] I left

[14] Oviedo, p. 587, has eight *or* nine days. On p. 586 he says they stayed 26 days at Apalachen, instead of 25, as Cabeza de Vaca.

[15] This may have been the Apalachicola, according to the French map.

on the following day in search of it, accompanied by the commissary, the captain Castillo, Andrés Dorantes, seven horsemen and fifty foot. We marched until sunset, reaching an inlet or arm of the sea, where we found plenty of oysters on which the people feasted, and we gave many thanks to God for bringing us there.

The next day I sent twenty men to reconnoiter the coast and explore it, who returned on the day following at nightfall, saying that these inlets and bays were very large and went so far inland as greatly to impede our investigations, and that the coast was still at a great distance. Hearing this and considering how ill-prepared we were for the task, I returned to where the Governor was. We found him sick, together with many others. The night before, Indians had made an attack, putting them in great stress, owing to their enfeebled condition. The Indians had also killed one of their horses. I reported upon my journey and on the bad condition of the country. That day we remained there.

ALVAR NUNEZ CABEZA DE VACA

ON the next day we left Aute and marched (all day) to the spot I had visited on my last exploration. Our march was extremely difficult, for neither had we horses enough to carry the sick, nor did we know how to relieve them. They became worse every day, and our sufferings were afflicting. There it became manifest how few resources we had for going further, and even in case we had been provided we did not know where to go; our men were mostly sick and too much out of condition to be of any use whatever. I refrain from making a long story of it. Any one can imagine what might be experienced in a land so strange and so utterly without resources of any kind, either for stay or for an escape. Nevertheless, since the surest aid was God, Our Lord, and since we never doubted of it, something happened that put us in a worse plight yet.

Most of the horsemen began to leave in secret, hoping thus to save themselves, forsaking the Governor and the sick, who were helpless.[16] Still, as among them were many of good families and of rank, they would not suffer this to happen unbeknown to the Governor and Your Majesty's officials, so that, when we remonstrated, showing at what an unseasonable time they were leaving their captain and the sick and, above all, forsaking Your Majesty's service, they concluded to stay, and share the fate of all, without abandoning one another. The Governor thereupon called them to his presence all together, and each one in particular, asking their opinion about this dismal country, so as to be able to get out of it and seek relief, for in that land there was none.

One-third of our people were dangerously ill, getting worse hourly, and we felt sure of meeting the same fate, with death as our only prospect, which in such a country was much worse yet. And considering these and many other inconveniences and that we had tried many expedients, we finally resorted to a very diffi-

[16]Of this planned desertion Oviedo says nothing.

cult one, which was to build some craft in which to leave the land. It seemed impossible, as none of us knew how to construct ships. We had no tools, no iron, no smithery, no oakum, no pitch, no tackling; finally, nothing of what was indispensable. Neither was there anybody to instruct us in shipbuilding, and, above all, there was nothing to eat, while the work was going on, for those who would have to perform the task. Considering all this, we agreed to think it over. Our parley ceased for that day, and everyone went off, leaving it to God, Our Lord, to put him on the right road according to His pleasure.

The next day God provided that one of the men should come, saying that he would make wooden flues, and bellows of deerskin, and as we were in such a state that anything appearing like relief seemed acceptable, we told him to go to work, and agreed to make of our stirrups, spurs, cross-bows and other iron implements the nails, saws and hatchets and other tools we so greatly needed for our purpose.

In order to obtain food while the work proposed was in progress we determined upon four successive raids into Aute, with all the horses and men that were fit for service, and that on every third day a horse should be killed and the meat distributed among those who worked at the barges and among the sick. The raids were executed with such people and horses as were able, and they brought as many as four hundred fanegas of maize, although not without armed opposition from the Indians. We gathered plenty of palmettos, using their fibre and husk, twisting and preparing it in place of oakum for the barges. The work on these was done by the only carpenter we had, and progressed so rapidly that, beginning on the fourth day of August, on the twentieth day of the month of September[17] five barges of twenty-two elbow lengths each were ready, caulked with palmetto oakum and tarred with pitch, which a Greek called Don Teodoro made from certain pines. Of the husk of pal-

[17]The latter date is also in Oviedo (p. 588), but not in *Relacion;* but the estimate of the distances is of little importance. It is a computation of the length of the line of march, not the distance between two points.

mettos, and of the tails and manes of the horses we made ropes and tackles, of our shirts sails, and of the junipers that grew there we made the oars, which we thought were necessary, and such was the stress in which our sins had placed us that only with very great trouble could we find stones for ballast and anchors of the barges, for we had not seen a stone in the whole country. We flayed the legs of the horses and tanned the skin to make leather pouches for carrying water.

During that time some of the party went to the coves and inlets for sea-food, and the Indians surprised them twice, killing ten of our men in plain view of the camp, without our being able to prevent it. We found them shot through and through with arrows, for, although several wore good armor, it was not sufficient to protect them, since, as I said before, they shot their arrows with such force and precision. According to the sworn statements of our pilots, we had travelled from the bay, to which we gave the name of the Cross, to this place, two hundred and eighty leagues, more or less.

In all these parts we saw no mountains nor heard of any, and before embarking we had lost over forty men through sickness and hunger, besides those killed by Indians. On the twenty-second day of the month of September we had eaten up all the horses but one. We embarked in the following order: In the barge of the Governor there were forty-nine men, and as many in the one entrusted to the purser and the commissary. The third barge he placed in charge of Captain Alonso del Castillo and of Andrés Dorantes, with forty-eight men; in another he placed two captains, named Tellez and Peñalosa, with forty-seven men. The last one he gave to the inspector and to me, with forty-nine men, and, after clothing and supplies were put on board, the sides of the barges only rose half a foot above the water. Besides, we were so crowded as to be unable to stir. So great is the power of need that it brought us to venture out into such a troublesome sea in this manner, and without any one among us having the least knowledge of the art of navigation.

THAT bay from which we started is called the Bay of the Horses. We sailed seven days among those inlets, in the water waist deep, without signs of anything like the coast. At the end of this time we reached an island near the shore. My barge went ahead, and from it we saw five Indian canoes coming. The Indians abandoned them and left them in our hands, when they saw that we approached. The other barges went on and saw some lodges on the same island, where we found plenty of ruffs and their eggs, dried, and that was a very great relief in our needy condition. Having taken them, we went further, and two leagues beyond found a strait between the island and the coast, which strait we christened Sant Miguel, it being the day of that saint. Issuing from it we reached the coast, where by means of the five canoes I had taken from the Indians we mended somewhat the barges, making washboards and adding to them and raising the sides two hands above water.

Then we set out to sea again, coasting towards the River of Palms.[19] Every day our thirst and hunger increased because our supplies were giving out, as well as the water supply, for the pouches we had made from the legs of our horses soon became rotten and useless. From time to time we would enter some inlet or cove that reached very far inland, but we found them all shallow and dangerous, and so we navigated through them for thirty days, meeting sometimes Indians who fished and were poor and wretched people.

At the end of these thirty days, and when we were in extreme need of water and hugging the coast, we heard one night a canoe approaching. When we saw it we stopped

[19]This "Rio de las Palmas" is frequently mentioned in the oldest sources on Florida and north-eastern Mexico. (See, concerning it, the expedition of De Soto in "*Trail-Makers.*") The map by Brevoort identifies the "Rio de las Palmas" with the Rio Grande. The mouth of the Palmas is stated to have been sixty leagues above (north) of that of the Pánuco river. This, as well as the statement repeatedly found in older documents, that from the river of Palms the coast turns to the south, whereas from Florida on it ran from east to west, favors the assumption.

and waited, but it would not come to us, and, although we called out, it would neither turn back nor wait. It being night, we did not follow the canoe, but proceeded. At dawn we saw a small island, where we touched to search for water, but in vain, as there was none. While at anchor a great storm overtook us. We remained there six days without venturing to leave, and it being five days since we had drank anything our thirst was so great as to compel us to drink salt water, and several of us took such an excess of it that we lost suddenly five men.

I tell this briefly, not thinking it necessary to relate in particular all the distress and hardships we bore. Moreover, if one takes into account the place we were in and the slight chances of relief he may imagine what we suffered. Seeing that our thirst was increasing and the water was killing us, while the storm did not abate, we agreed to trust to God, Our Lord, and rather risk the perils of the sea than wait there for certain death from thirst. So we left in the direction we had seen the canoe going on the night we came here. During this day we found ourselves often on the verge of drowning and so forlorn that there was none in our company who did not expect to die at any moment.

It was Our Lord's pleasure, who many a time shows His favor in the hour of greatest distress, that at sunset we turned a point of land and found there shelter and much improvement. Many canoes came and the Indians in them spoke to us, but turned back without waiting. They were tall and well built, and carried neither bows nor arrows. We followed them to their lodges, which were nearly along the inlet, and landed, and in front of the lodges we saw many jars with water, and great quantities of cooked fish. The chief of that land offered all to the Governor and led him to his abode. The dwellings were of matting and seemed to be permanent. When we entered the home of the chief he gave us plenty of fish, while we gave him of our maize, which they ate in our presence, asking for more. So we gave more to them, and the Governor presented him with some trinkets. While with the cacique at his lodge, half an hour after sunset, the Indians suddenly fell upon us and upon our sick people on the beach.

They also attacked the house of the cacique, where the Governor was, wounding him in the face with a stone. Those who were with him seized the cacique, but as his people were so near he escaped, leaving in our hands a robe of marten-ermine skin, which, I believe, are the finest in the world and give out an odor like amber and musk. A single one can be smelt so far off that it seems as if there were a great many. We saw more of that kind, but none like these.

Those of us who were there, seeing the Governor hurt, placed him aboard the barge and provided that most of the men should follow him to the boats. Some fifty of us remained on land to face the Indians, who attacked thrice that night, and so furiously as to drive us back every time further than a strone's throw.

Not one of us escaped unhurt. I was wounded in the face, and if they had had more arrows (for only a few were found) without any doubt they would have done us great harm. At the last onset the Captains Dorantes, Peñalosa and Tellez, with fifteen men, placed themselves in ambush and attacked them from the rear, causing them to flee and leave us. The next morning I destroyed more than thirty of their canoes, which served to protect us against a northern wind then blowing, on account of which we had to stay there, in the severe cold, not venturing out to sea on account of the heavy storm. After this we again embarked and navigated for three days, having taken along but a small supply of water, the vessels we had for it being few. So we found ourselves in the same plight as before.

Continuing onward, we entered a firth and there saw a canoe with Indians approaching. As we hailed them they came, and the Governor, whose barge they neared first, asked them for water. They offered to get some, provided we gave them something in which to carry it, and a Christian Greek, called Doroteo Teodoro (who has already been mentioned), said he would go with them. The Governor and others vainly tried to dissuade him, but he insisted upon going and went, taking along a negro, while the Indians left two of their number as hostages. At night the Indians returned and brought back our vessels, but without water; neither did the Christians return with them. Those that had remained as hostages, when their people spoke to them, attempted to throw themselves into the water. But our men in the barge held them back, and so the other Indians forsook their canoe, leaving us very despondent and sad for the loss of those two Christians.

IN the morning many canoes of Indians came, demanding their two companions, who had remained in the barge as hostages. The Governor answered that he would give them up, provided they returned the two Christians. With those people there came five or six chiefs, who seemed to us to be of better appearance, greater authority and manner of composure than any we had yet seen, although not as tall as those of whom we have before spoken. They wore the hair loose and very long, and were clothed in robes of marten, of the kind we had obtained previously, some of them done up in a very strange fashion, because they showed patterns of fawn-colored furs that looked very well.

They entreated us to go with them, and said that they would give us the Christians, water and many other things, and more canoes kept coming towards us, trying to block the mouth of that inlet, and for this reason, as well as because the land appeared very dangerous to remain in, we took again to sea, where we stayed with them till noon. And as they would not return the Christians, and for that reason neither would we give up the Indians, they began to throw stones at us with slings, and darts, threatening to shoot arrows, although we did not see more than three or four bows.

While thus engaged the wind freshened and they turned about and left us. We navigated that day until nightfall, when my bark, which was the foremost, discovered a promontory made by the coast. At the other end was a very large river, and at a small island on the point I anchored to wait for the other barges.

The Governor did not want to touch, but entered a bay close by, where there were many small islands. There we got together and took fresh water out of the sea, because the river emptied into it like a torrent.

For two days we had eaten the corn raw, and now, in order to toast it, we went ashore on that island, but not finding any firewood, agreed to go to the river, which was one league from there behind the point. However, the current was so strong that it in no way allowed us to land, but rather carried us away from the shore against all our efforts. The north wind that blew off shore freshened so much that it drove us back to the high sea, without our being able to do anything against it, and at about one-half league from shore we sounded and found no bottom even at thirty fathoms. Without being able to understand it, it was the current that disturbed our soundings. We navigated two days yet, trying hard to reach the shore. On the third day, a little before sunrise, we saw many columns of smoke rising on the coast. Working towards these, we found ourselves in three fathoms of water, but it being night did not dare to land because, as we had seen so much smoke, we believed that greater danger might be in wait for us there. We were unable to see, owing to the darkness, what we should do. So we determined to wait until morning.

When it dawned the barges had been driven apart from each other. I found myself in thirty fathoms and, drifting along at the hour of vespers, I descried two barges, and as I approached saw that the first one was that of the Governor, who asked me what I thought we should do. I told him that we ought to rejoin the other barge, which was ahead of us, and in no manner forsake her, and the three together should continue our way whither God might take us. He replied it was impossible, since the barge was drifting far away into the sea, whereas he wanted to land, but that if I wished to follow I should put the people of my barge at the oars and work hard, as only by the strength of our arms the land could be reached. In this he had been advised by a captain he had along, whose name was Pantoja, who told him that if he did not land that day he would not in six days more, during which time we would of necessity starve.

Seeing his determination, I took to my own oar and the other oarsmen in my craft did the same, and thus we rowed until nearly sunset. But as the Governor had with him the healthiest and strongest men, in no way could we follow or keep up with him. Seeing this, I asked him to give me a rope from his barge to be able to follow, but he answered that it was no small effort on their part alone to reach the shore on that night. I told him that since it was barely possible for us to follow and do what he had ordained, he should tell me what he commanded me to do. He answered that this was no time for orders; that each one should do the best he could to save himself; that he intended to do it that way, and with this he went on with his craft[20]

As I could not follow him, I went after the other barge, which was out at sea and waited for me, and reaching it I found it was the one of the Captains Peñalosa and Tellez. We travelled together for four days, our daily ration being half a handful of raw maize. At the end of these four days a storm overtook us, in which the other barge was lost.[21] God's great mercy preserved us from being drowned in that weather.

It being winter and the cold very great, and as we had been suffering so many days from hunger and from the injuries we received from the waves, that the next day people began to break down, so that when

[20]The conduct of Narvaez is justly criticised by Oviedo (Vol. III, p. 590). The Letter to the Audiencia mentions it, and *Relacion* (p. 275) alludes to it simply.

[21]*Relacion* (p. 275) mentions the loss of the barge of Tellez and Peñalosa. The text of Oviedo (III, p. 590) is quite different. What Cabeza de Vaca states happened four days after the meeting; the Letter to the Audiencia refers to the day immediately after. It barely alludes to the loss of the barge of Peñalosa, &c. This discrepancy seems to have escaped Oviedo himself, since he does not speak of it in Chapter VII (p. 614, &c.).

the sun set all those aboard of my barge had fallen in a heap and were so near dying that few remained conscious, and not five men kept on their feet.

When night came the skipper and I were the only ones able to manage the barge. Two hours after nightfall the skipper told me to steer the craft alone, since he felt that he would die that same night. Thereupon I stood at the helm, and after midnight went to see if the skipper was dead, but he said that, on the contrary, he felt better and would steer till daybreak. On that occasion I would have hailed death with delight rather than to see so many people around me in such a condition. After the skipper had taken the barge under his control I went to rest, very much without resting, for I thought of anything else but sleep.

Near daybreak I fancied to hear the sound of breakers, for as the coast was low, their noise was greater. Surprised at it, I called the skipper, who said he thought we were near the shore. Sounding, we found seven fathoms, and he was of the opinion that we should keep off shore till dawn. So I took the oar and rowed along the coast, from which we were one league away, and turned the stern to seaward.

Close to shore a wave took us and hurled the barge a horse's length out of water. With the violent shock nearly all the people who lay in the boat like dead came to themselves, and, seeing we were close to land, began to crawl out on all fours. As they took to some rocks, we built a fire and toasted some of our maize. We found rain water, and with the warmth of the fire people revived and began to cheer up. The day we arrived there was the sixth of the month of November.

AFTER the people had eaten I sent Lope de Oviedo, who was the strongest and heartiest of all, to go to some trees nearby and climb to the top of one, examine the surroundings and the country in which we were. He did so and found we were on an island, and that the ground was hollowed out, as if cattle had gone over it, from which it seemed to him that the land belonged to Christians, and so he told us. I sent him again to look and examine more closely if there were any worn trails, and not to go too far so as not to run into danger. He went, found a footpath, followed it for about one-half league, and saw several Indian huts which stood empty because the Indians had gone out into the field.[22]

He took away a cooking pot, a little dag and a few ruffs and turned back, but as he seemed to delay I sent two other Christians to look for him and find out what had happened.

They met him nearby and saw that three Indians, with bows and arrows, were following and calling to him, while he did the same to them by signs. So he came to where we were, the Indians remaining behind, seated on the beach. Half an hour after a hundred Indian archers joined them, and our fright was such that, whether tall or little, it made them appear

[22]The word *"campo"* means literally field, but in the present instance may as well apply to the surrounding country in general, whether level or accidented, wooded or a grassy plain. The idea of cultivated land is, of course excluded.

giants to us. They stood still close to the first ones, near where we were.

We could not defend ourselves, as there were scarcely three of us who could stand on their feet. The inspector and I stepped forward and called them. They came, and we tried to quiet them the best we could and save ourselves, giving them beads and bells. Each one of them gave me an arrow in token of friendship, and by signs they gave us to understand that on the following morning they would come back with food, as then they had none.

THE next day, at sunrise, which was the hour the Indians had given us to understand, they came as promised and brought us plenty of fish and some roots which they eat that taste like nuts, some bigger, some smaller, most of which are taken out of the water with much trouble.

In the evening they returned and brought us more fish and some of the same roots, and they brought their women and children to look at us. They thought themselves very rich with the little bells and beads we gave them, and thereafter visited us daily with the same things as before. As we saw ourselves provided with fish, roots, water and the other things we had asked for, we concluded to embark again and continue our voyage.

We lifted the barge out of the sand into which it had sunk (for which purpose we all had to take off our clothes) and had great work to set her afloat, as our condition was such that much lighter things would have given us trouble.

Then we embarked. Two crossbow shots from shore a wave swept over us, we all got wet, and being naked and the cold very great, the oars dropped out of our hands. The next wave overturned the barge. The inspector and two others clung to her to save themselves, but the contrary happened; they got underneath the barge and were drowned.

The shore being very rough, the sea took the others and thrust them, half dead, on the beach of the same island again, less the three that had perished underneath the barge.

The rest of us, as naked as we had been born, had lost everything, and while it was not worth much, to us it meant a great deal. It was in November, bitterly cold, and we in such a state that every bone could easily be counted, and we looked like death itself. Of myself I can say that since the month of May I had not tasted anything but toasted maize, and even sometimes had been obliged to eat it raw. Although the horses were killed during the time the barges were built, I never could eat of them, and not ten times did I taste fish. This I say in order to explain and that any one might guess how we were off. On top of all this, a north wind arose, so that we were nearer death than life. It pleased Our Lord that, searching for the remnants of our former fire, we found wood with which we built big fires and then with many tears begged Our Lord for mercy and forgiveness of our sins. Every one of us pitied not only himself, but all the others whom he saw in the same condition.

At sunset the Indians, thinking we had not left, came to bring us food, but when they saw us in such a different attire from before and so strange-looking, they were so frightened as to turn back. I went to call them, and in great fear they came. I then gave them to understand by signs how we had lost a barge and three of our men had been drowned, while before them there lay two of our men dead, with the others about to go the same way.

Upon seeing the disaster we had suffered, our misery and distress, the Indians sat down with us and all began to weep out of compassion for our misfortune, and for more than half an hour they wept so loud and so sincerely that it could be heard far away.

Verily, to see beings so devoid of reason, untutored, so like unto brutes, yet so deeply moved by pity for us, it increased my feelings and those of others in my company for our own misfortune. When the lament was over, I spoke to the Christians and asked them if they would like me to beg the Indians to take us to their homes. Some of the men, who had been to New Spain, answered that it would be unwise, as, once at their abode, they might sacrifice us to their idols.

Still, seeing there was no remedy and that in any other way death was surer and nearer, I did not mind what they said, but begged the Indians to take us to their dwellings, at which they showed great pleasure, telling us to tarry yet a little, but that they would do what we wished. Soon thirty of them loaded themselves with firewood and went to their lodges, which were far away, while we stayed with the others until it was almost dark. Then they took hold of us and carried us along hurriedly to where they lived.

Against the cold, and lest on the way some one of us might faint or die, they had provided four or five big fires on the road, at each one of which they warmed us. As soon as they saw we had regained a little warmth and strength they would carry us to the next fire with such haste that our feet barely touched the ground.

So we got to their dwellings, where we

saw they had built a hut for us with many fires in it. About one hour after our arrival they began to dance and to make a great celebration (which lasted the whole night), although there was neither pleasure, feast nor sleep in it for us, since we expected to be sacrificed. In the morning they again gave us fish and roots, and treated us so well that we became reassured, losing somewhat our apprehension of being butchered.

THAT same day I saw on one of the Indians a trinket he had not gotten from us, and asking from where they had obtained it they answered, by signs, that other men like ourselves and who were still in our rear, had given it to them. Hearing this, I sent two Christians with two Indians to guide them to those people. Very near by they met them, and they also were looking for us, as the Indians had told them of our presence in the neighborhood. These were the Captains Andrés Dorantes and Alonso del Castillo, with all of their crew. When they came near us they were much frightened at our appearance and grieved at being unable to give us anything, since they had nothing but their clothes. And they stayed with us there, telling how, on the fifth of that same month, their barge stranded a league and a half from there, and they escaped without anything being lost.

All together, we agreed upon repairing their barge, and that those who had strength and inclination should proceed in it, while the others should remain until completely restored and then go as best they could along the coast, following it till God would be pleased to get us all together to a land of Christians.

So we set to work, but ere the barge was afloat Tavera, a gentleman in our company, died, while the barge proved not to be seaworthy and soon sank. Now, being in the condition which I have stated—that is, most of us naked and the weather so unfavorable for walking and for swimming across rivers and coves, and we had neither food nor any way to carry it, we determined upon submitting to necessity and upon wintering there, and we also agreed that four men, who were the most able-bodied, should go to Pánuco, which we believed to be nearby, and that, if it was God, Our Lord's will to take them there, they should tell of our remaining on the island and of our distress. One of them was a Portuguese, called Alvaro Fernandez, a carpenter and sailor; the second was Mendez; the third, Figueroa, a native of Toledo; the fourth, Astudillo, from Zafra. They were all good swimmers and took with them an Indian from the island.

A FEW days after these four Christians had left, the weather became so cold and tempestuous that the Indians could no longer pull roots, and the canebrake in which they used to fish yielded nothing more. As the lodges afforded so little shelter, people began to die, and five Christians, quartered on the coast, were driven to such an extremity that they atc each other up until but one remained, who being left alone, there was nobody to eat him. Their names are: Sierra, Diego,

Lopez, Corral, Palacios and Gonzalo Ruiz. At this the Indians were so startled, and there was such an uproar among them, that I verily believe if they had seen this at the beginning they would have killed them, and we all would have been in great danger. After a very short time, out of eighty men who had come there in our two parties only fifteen remained alive.

Then the natives fell sick from the stomach, so that one-half of them died also, and they, believing we had killed them, and holding it to be certain, they agreed among themselves to kill those of us who survived.

But when they came to execute it an Indian who kept me told them not to believe we were the cause of their dying, for if we had so much power we would not have suffered so many of our own people to perish without being able to remedy it ourselves. He also told them there remained but very few of us, and none of them did any harm or injury, so that the best was to let us alone. It pleased Our Lord they should listen to his advice and counsel and give up their idea.

To this island we gave the name of the *Island of Ill Fate.*[23] The people on it are tall and well formed; they have no other weapons than bows and arrows with which they are most dextrous. The men have one of their nipples perforated from side to side and sometimes both; through this hole is thrust a reed as long as two and a half hands and as thick as two fingers; they also have the under lip perforated and a piece of cane in it as thin as the half of a finger. The women do the hard work. People stay on this island from October till the end of February, feeding on the roots I have mentioned, taken from under the water in November and December. They have channels made of reeds and get fish only during that time; afterwards they subsist on roots. At the end of February they remove to other parts in search of food, because the roots begin to sprout and are not good any more.

Of all the people in the world, they are those who most love their children and treat

[23]In *Relacion* (p. 277) Cabeza de Vaca says the island was called by them *"Mal Fondo,"* which seems a misprint.

them best, and should the child of one of them happen to die, parents and relatives bewail it, and the whole settlement, the lament lasting a full year, day after day. Before sunrise the parents begin to weep, after them the tribe, and the same they do at noon and at dawn. At the end of the year of mourning they celebrate the anniversary and wash and cleanse themselves of all their paint. They mourn all their dead in this manner, old people excepted, to whom they do not pay any attention, saying that these have had their time and are no longer of any use, but only take space, and food from the children.

Their custom is to bury the dead, except those who are medicine men among them, whom they burn, and while the fire is burning, all dance and make a big festival, grinding the bones to powder. At the end of the year, when they celebrate the anniversary, they scarify themselves and give to the relatives the pulverized bones to drink in water. Every man has a recognized wife, but the medicine men enjoy greater privileges, since they may have two or three, and among these wives there is great friendship and harmony.

When one takes a woman for his wife, from the day he marries her, whatever he may hunt or fish, she has to fetch it to the home of her father, without daring to touch or eat of it, and from the home of the father-in-law they bring the food to the husband. All the while neither the wife's father nor her mother enter his abode, nor is he allowed to go to theirs, or to the homes of his brothers-in-law, and should they happen to meet they go out of each other's way a crossbow's shot or so, with bowed heads and eyes cast to the ground, holding it to be an evil thing to look at each other or speak. The women are free to communicate with their parents-in-law or relatives and speak to them. This custom prevails from that island as far as about fifty leagues inland.

There is another custom, that when a son or brother dies no food is gathered by those of his household for three months, preferring rather to starve, but the relatives and neighbors provide them with victuals. Now, as during the time we were there so many of them died, there was great starvation in most of the lodges, due to their customs and ceremonials, as well as to the weather, which was so rough that such as could go out after food brought in but very little, withal working hard for it. Therefore the Indians by whom I was kept forsook the island and in several canoes went over to the mainland to some bays where there were a great many oysters and during three months of the year they do not eat anything else and drink very bad water. There is lack of firewood, but great abundance of mosquitoes. Their lodges are made of matting and built on oyster shells, upon which they sleep in hides, which they only get by chance. There we remained to the end of April, when we went to the seashore, where we ate blackberries for a whole month, during which time they danced and celebrated incessantly.

ON the island I have spoken of they wanted to make medicine men of us without any examination or asking for our diplomas, because they cure diseases by breathing on the sick, and with that breath and their hands they drive the ailment away. So they summoned us to do the same in order to be at least of some use. We laughed, taking it for a jest, and said that we did not understand how to cure.

Thereupon they withheld our food to compel us to do what they wanted. Seeing our obstinacy, an Indian told me that I did not know what I said by claiming that what he knew was useless, because stones and things growing out in the field have their virtues, and he, with a heated stone, placing it on the stomach, could cure and take away pain, so that we, who were wiser men, surely had greater power and virtue.

At last we found ourselves in such stress as to have to do it, without risking any punishment. Their manner of curing is as follows: When one is ill they call in a medicine man, and after they are well again not only do they give him all they have, but even things they strive to obtain from their relatives. All the medicine man does is to make a few cuts where the pain is located and then suck the skin around the incisions. They cauterize with fire, thinking it very effective, and I found it to be so by my own experience. Then they breathe on the spot where the pain is and believe that with this the disease goes away.[24]

The way we treated the sick was to make over them the sign of the cross while breathing on them, recite a Pater noster and Ave Maria, and pray to God, Our Lord, as best we could to give them good health and inspire them to do us some favors. Thanks to His will and the mercy He had upon us, all those for whom we prayed, as soon as we crossed them, told the others that they were cured and felt well again. For this they gave us good cheer, and would rather be without food themselves so as to give it to us, and they gave us hides and other small things. So great was the lack of food

[24]Jacques le Moyne de Morgues, *Brevis Narratio corvm quæ in Florida Americæ Provicia Gallis acciderunt* (1591, in De Bry), says of the "Mode of treating the sick" (*Narrative of Le Moyne,* Illustration 20, p. 9): "Cutting into the skin of the forehead with a sharp shell, they suck out blood with their mouths." The remainder of the ceremony, as described, differs from that related by Cabeza de Vaca.

then that I often remained without eating anything whatsoever for three days, and they were in the same plight, so that it seemed to me impossible for life to last, although I afterwards suffered still greater privations and much more distress, as I shall tell further on.

The Indians that kept Alonso del Castillo, Andrés Dorantes and the others, who were still alive, being of another language and stock, had gone to feed on oysters at another point of the mainland, where they remained until the first day of the month of April. Then they came back to the island, which was from there nearly two leagues off, where the channel is broadest. The island is half a league wide and five long.

All the people of this country go naked; only the women cover part of their bodies with a kind of wool that grows on trees. The girls go about in deer skins. They are very liberal towards each other with what they have. There is no ruler among them. All who are of the same descendancy cluster together. There are two distinct languages spoken on the island; those of one language are called Capoques, those of the other Han. They have the custom, when they know each other and meet from time to time, before they speak, to weep for half an hour. After they have wept the one who receives the visit rises and gives to the other all he has. The other takes it, and in a little while goes away with everything. Even sometimes, after having given and obtained all, they part without having uttered a word. There are other very queer customs, but having told the principal ones and the most striking, I must now proceed to relate what further happened to us.

AFTER Dorantes and Castillo had come back to the island, they gathered together all the Christians, who were somewhat scattered, and there were in all fourteen. I, as told, was in another place, on the mainland, whither my Indians had taken me and where I suffered from such a severe illness that, although I might otherwise have entertained some hope for life, this was enough to take it away from me completely. When the Christians learned of it they gave an Indian the robe of marten we had taken from the cacique, as stated, in order that he should guide them to where I was, to see me, and so twelve of them came, two having become so feeble that they did not dare to take them along.

The names of those who came are: Alonso del Castillo, Andrés Dorantes and Diego Dorantes, Valdivieso, Estrada, Tostado, Chaves, Gutierrez, an Asturian priest; Diego de Huelva, Estevanico, the negro Benitez, and as they reached the mainland they found still another of our men named Francisco de Léon, and the thirteen went along the coast. After they had gone by, the Indians with whom I was told me of it, and how Hiéronimo de Alaniz and Lope de Oviedo had been left on the island.

My sickness prevented me from following or seeing them. I had to remain with those same Indians of the island for more than one year, and as they made me work so much and treated me so badly I determined to flee and go to those who live in the woods on the mainland, and who are called those from (of) Charruco.

I could no longer stand the life I was compelled to lead. Among many other troubles I had to pull the eatable roots out of the water and from among the canes where they were buried in the ground, and from this my fingers had become so tender that the mere touch of a straw caused them to bleed. The reeds would cut me in many places, because many were broken and I had to go in among them with the clothing I had on, of which I have told. This is why I went to work and joined the other Indians. Among these I improved my condition a little by becoming a trader, doing the best in it I could, and they gave me food and treated me well.

They entreated me to go about from one part to another to get the things they needed, as on account of constant warfare there is neither travel nor barter in the land.

So, trading along with my wares I penetrated inland as far as I cared to go and along the coast as much as forty or fifty leagues. My stock consisted mainly of pieces of seashells and cockles, and shells with which they cut a fruit which is like a bean, used by them for healing and in their dances and feasts. This is of greatest value among them, besides shell-beads and other objects. These things I carried inland, and in exchange brought back hides and red ochre with which they rub and dye their faces and hair; flint for arrow points, glue and hard canes wherewith to make them, and tassels made of the hair of deer, which they dye red. This trade suited me well because it gave me liberty to go wherever I pleased; I was not bound to do anything and no longer a slave. Wherever I went they treated me well, and gave me to eat for the sake of my wares. My principal object in doing it, however, was to find out in what manner I might get further away. I became well known among them; they rejoiced greatly when seeing me and I would bring them what they needed, and those who did not know me would desire and endeavor to meet me for the sake of my fame.

My sufferings, while trading thus, it

would take long to tell; danger, hunger, storms and frost overtaking me often in the open field and alone, and from which through the mercy of God, Our Lord, I escaped. For this reason I did not go out trading in winter, it being the time when the Indians themselves remain in their huts and abodes, unable to go out or assist each other.

Nearly six years I spent thus in the country, alone among them and naked, as they all were themselves.

The reason for remaining so long was that I wished to take with me a Christian called Lope de Oviedo, who still lingered on the island. The other companion, Alaniz, who remained with him after Alonso del Castillo and Andrés Dorantes and all the others had gone, soon died, and in order to get him (Oviedo) out of there, I went over to the island every year, entreating him to leave with me and go, as well as we could, in search of Christians. But year after year he put it off to the year that was to follow. In the end I got him to come, took him away, and carried him across the inlets and through four rivers on the coast, since he could not swim. Thence we proceeded, together with several Indians, to an inlet one league wide, very deep everywhere and which seemed to us, from what we saw, to be the one called of the Holy Ghost.[25]

On the opposite shore we saw Indians who had come to meet those in our company. They informed us that further on there were three men like ourselves and told us their names. Upon being asked about the rest of the party, they answered that all had died from cold and hunger and that the Indians beyond had killed Diego Dorantes, Valdivieso and Diego de Huelva wilfully, only because these had gone from one house to another, and their neighbors with whom was now the Captain Dorantes, had, in consequence of some dream dreamt by these Indians, killed Esquivel and Mendez also.

[25]"Espiritu Santo." This was the name given to a bay, and probably to the mouth of a large river. The Letter to the Audiencia, Oviedo (p. 593), describes it as follows: "This inlet (or bay) was wide, almost a league across, and it makes a point toward the direction of Pánuco, that juts out into the sea nearly a quarter of a league, with some great dunes of white sand visible at a great distance from the sea; and from this they suspected that it must have been the Espiritu Santo river."

We asked them about those who remained alive, and they said they were in a very sorry condition, as the boys and other Indians, idlers and roughs, kicked them, slapped their faces and beat them with sticks, and such was the life they had to lead.

We inquired about the country further on and the sustenance that might be found in it. They said it was very thinly settled, with nothing to eat, and the people dying from cold, as they had neither hides nor anything else to protect their bodies. They also told us that, if we wished to meet the three Christians about two days hence, the Indians would come to a place about a league from there on the shore of that river to feed on nuts. And to show us that what they said of the ill-treatment of our people was true the Indians with whom we were kicked and beat my companion. Neither did I remain without my share of it. They threw mud at us, and put arrows to our chests every day, saying they would kill us in the same way as our other companions. And fearing this, Lope de Oviedo, my companion, said he preferred to go back, with some women of the Indians in whose company we had forded the cove and who had remained behind. I insisted he should not go and did all I could to prevail upon him to remain, but it was in vain. He went back and I remained alone among these Indians, who are named *Guevenes,* whereas those with whom he went away were called *Deaguanes.*

TWO days after Lope de Oviedo had gone the Indians who kept Alonso del Castillo and Andrés Dorantes came to the very spot we had been told of to eat the nuts upon which they subsist for two months in the year, grinding certain small grains with them, without eating anything else. Even of that they do not always have, since one year there may be some and the next year not. They (the nuts) are of the size of those of Galicia, and the trees are very big and numerous.

An Indian told me that the Christians had come and that if I wished to see them

I should run away to hide on the edge of a grove to which he pointed, as he and some of his relatives were to visit these Indians and would take me along to the Christians. I confided in them and determined to do it because they spoke a different language from that of my Indians. So the next day they took me along. When I got near the site where they had their lodges, Andrés Dorantes came out to look who it was, because the Indians had informed him also that a Christian was coming, and when he saw me he was much frightened, as for many days they believed me to be dead, the Indians having told them so. We gave many thanks to God for being together again, and that day was one of the happiest we enjoyed in our time, and going to where was Castillo they asked me whither I went. I told him my purpose was to go to a country of Christians and that I followed this direction and trail. Andrés Dorantes said that for many days he had been urging Castillo and Estevanico to go further on, but they did not risk it, being unable to swim and afraid of the rivers and inlets that had to be crossed so often in that country.

Still, as it pleased God, Our Lord, to spare me after all my sufferings and sickness and finally let me rejoin them, they at last determined upon fleeing, as I would take them safely across the rivers and bays we might meet. But they advised me to keep it secret from the Indians (as well as my own departure) lest they would kill me forthwith, and that to avoid this it was necessary to remain with them for six months longer, after which time they would remove to another section in order to eat prickly pears. These are a fruit of the size of eggs, red and black, and taste very good. For three months they subsist upon them exclusively, eating nothing else.

Now, at the time they pluck this fruit, other Indians from beyond come to them with bows for barter and exchange, and when those turn back we thought of joining them and escaping in this way. With this understanding I remained, and they gave me as a slave to an Indian with whom Dorantes stayed. This Indian, his wife, their son and another Indian who was with them were all cross-eyed. These are called *Mariames*, and Castillo was with others, who were their neighbors, called *Iguaces*.

And so, being here with them, they told me that after leaving the Island of Ill-Fate they met on the coast the boat in which the purser and the monks were going adrift, and that crossing the rivers, of which there were four, all very large and very swift, the barges in which they crossed were swept out into the sea, where four of their number were drowned. Thus they went ahead until they had crossed the inlet, which they did by dint of great efforts. Fifteen leagues from there they met another of our parties, and when they reached there, already two of their companions had died in sixty leagues of travel. The survivors also were very near death. On the whole trip they ate nothing but crawfish and *yerba pedrera*.[26]

At this, the last cove, they said they saw Indians eating blackberries, who, upon perceiving the Christians, went away to an-

[26] I have been unable to find, as yet, any reference that might serve to explain this term.

other promontory. While seeking a way to cross the cove an Indian and a Christian came towards them, and they recognized Figueroa, one of the four we had sent ahead from the Island of Ill-Fate, who there told them how he and his companions had gotten to that place, where two of their number and one Indian had died from cold and hunger, because they had come and remained in the worst weather known. He also said the Indians took him and Mendez.

While with them Mendez fled, going in the direction of Pánuco as best he might, but the Indians pursued and killed him. So, as he (Figueroa) was with these same Indians he learned (from them) that with the *Mariames* there was a Christian who had come over from the other side and had met him[27] with those called *Guevenes;* and that this Christian was Hernando de Esquivel, from Badajoz, a companion of the commissary. From Esquivel he learned how the Governor, the purser and the others had ended.

[27]Thus in original, although it seems unclear. I do not venture to make or suggest a change.

The purser, with the friars, had stranded with their barge among the rivers, and, while they were proceeding along the coast, the barge of the Governor and his men came to land also. He (the Governor) then went with his barge as far as the big cove, whence he returned and took his men across to the other side, then came back for the purser, the monks and the rest. He further told him that after disembarking, the Governor revoked the powers he had given to the purser as his lieutenant, giving the office to a captain that was with him called Pantoja.

The Governor did not land that night, but remained on his barge with a pilot and a page who was sick. They had neither water nor anything to eat aboard, and at midnight a northerner set in with such violence that it carried the barge out into the sea, without anybody noticing it. They had for an anchor only a stone, and never more did they hear of him. Thereupon the people who had remained on land proceeded along the coast, and, being much impeded by water, built rafts with great trouble, in which they passed to the other side.

Going ahead, they reached a point of timber on the beach, where they found Indians, who, upon seeing them approach, placed their lodges on the canoes and crossed over to the other side of the coast, and the Christians, in view of the season and weather, since it was in the month of November, remained in this timber, because they found water and firewood, some crawfish and other sea-food, but from cold and hunger they began to die.

Moreover, Pantoja, who remained as lieutenant, ill-treated them. On this Sotomayor, brother of Vasco Porcallo (the one from the Island of Cuba, who had come in the fleet as Maestro de Campo), unable to stand it longer, quarrelled with Pantoja and struck him a blow with a stick, of which he died. Thus they perished one after another, the survivors slicing the dead for meat. The last one to die was Sotomayor, and Esquivel cut him up and fed on his body until the first of March, when an Indian, of those who had taken to flight previously, came to look if they were dead and took Esquivel along with him.

Once in the hands of this Indian, Figueroa spoke to Esquivel, learning from him what we have told here, and he entreated him to go in his company towards Pánuco. But Esquivel refused, saying he had heard from the monks that Pánuco was in their rear, and so he remained, while Figueroa went back to the coast where he formerly had been.[28]

ALL this account Figueroa gave after Esquivel's narrative, and thus, from one to the other, it came to me. Through it the fate of the whole fleet will be learned and known, and what happened to every one in particular. And he said furthermore that if the Christians would go about there for some time they might possibly meet Esquivel, because he knew that he had run away from the Indian with whom he was and gone to others called *Mariames,* who were their neighbors. And, as I have

[28]This is substantially corroborated in Oviedo.

just said, he and the Asturian wished to go to other Indians further on, but when those with whom they were found it out, they beat them severely, undressed the Asturian and pierced one of his arms with an arrow.

At last the Christians escaped through flight, and remained with the other Indians, whose slaves they agreed to become. But, although serving them, they were so ill-treated, that no slaves, nor men in any condition of life, were ever so abused. Not content with cuffing and beating them and pulling out their beards for mere pastime, they killed three out of the six only because they went from one lodge to another. These were Diego Dorantes, Valdivieso and Diego de Huelva. The three remaining ones expected to meet the same fate in the end.

To escape from that life Andrés Dorantes fled to the *Mariames*, and they were the ones with whom Esquivel had been. They told him how Esquivel stayed with them and how he fled because a woman dreamt he would kill her son, and the Indians pursued and killed him. They also showed Andrés Dorantes his sword, his rosary, his prayer book and other things of his.

It is a custom of theirs to kill even their own children for the sake of dreams, and the girls when newly born they throw away to be eaten by dogs. The reason why they do it is (as they say) that all the others of that country are their enemies with whom they are always at war, and should they marry their daughters they might multiply so much as to be able to overcome them and reduce them to slavery. Hence they prefer to kill the girls rather than see them give birth to children who would become their foes.

We asked them why they did not wed the girls among themselves. They replied it was bad to marry them to their own kin, and much better to do away with their daughters than to leave them to relatives or to enemies. This custom they have in common with their neighbors, the *Iguaces,* and no other tribe of that country has it. When they want to get married they buy their wives from their enemies. The price paid for a woman is a bow, the best to be had, with two arrows, and if he has no bow he gives a net as much as a fathom in width and one in length. They kill their own children and buy those of strangers. Marriage only lasts as long as they please. For a mere nothing they break up wedlock.

Dorantes remained only a few days with those Indians and then escaped. Castillo and Estevanico went inland to the *Iguaces.* All those people are archers and well built, although not as tall as those we had left behind us, and they have the nipple and lip perforated. Their principal food are two or three kinds of roots, which they hunt for all over the land; they are very unhealthy, inflating, and it takes two days to roast them. Many are very bitter, and with all that they are gathered with difficulty. But those people are so much exposed to starvation that these roots are to them indispensable and they walk two and three leagues to obtain them. Now and then they kill deer and at times get a fish, but this is so little and their hunger so great that they eat spiders and ant eggs,[29] worms, lizards and

[29]The pupas.

salamanders and serpents, also vipers the bite of which is deadly. They swallow earth and wood, and all they can get, the dung of deer and more things I do not mention; and I verily believe, from what I saw, that if there were any stones in the country they would eat them also. They preserve the bones of the fish they eat, of snakes and other animals, to pulverize them and eat the powder.

The men do not carry burdens or loads, the women and old men have to do it, for those are the people they least esteem. They have not as much love for their children as those spoken of before. Some among them are given to unnatural vices. The women are compelled to do very hard work and in a great many ways, for out of twenty-four hours of day and night they get only six hours rest. They spend most of the night in stirring the fire to dry those roots which they eat, and at daybreak they begin to dig and carry firewood and water to their houses and attend to other necessary matters. Most of these Indians are great thieves, for, although very liberal towards each other, as soon as one turns his head, his own son or the father grabs what he can. They are great liars and drunkards and take something in order to become intoxicated. They are so accustomed to running that, without resting or getting tired, they run from morning till night in pursuit of a deer, and kill a great many, because they follow until the game is worn out, sometimes catching it alive. Their huts are of matting placed over four arches. They carry them on their back and move every two or three days in quest of food; they plant nothing that would be of any use.

They are a very merry people, and even when famished do not cease to dance and celebrate their feasts and ceremonials. Their best times are when "tunas" (prickly pears) are ripe, because then they have plenty to eat and spend the time in dancing and eating day and night. As long as these tunas last the squeeze and open them and set them to dry. When dried they are put in baskets like figs and kept to be eaten on the way. The peelings they grind and pulverize.

While with them it happened many times

that we were three or four days without food. Then, in order to cheer us, they would tell us not to despair, since we would have tunas very soon and eat much and drink their juice and get big stomachs and be merry, contented and without hunger. But from the day they said it to the season of the tunas there would still elapse five or six months, and we had to wait that long.

When the time came, and we went to eat tunas, there were a great many mosquitoes of three kinds, all very bad and troublesome, which during most of the summer persecuted us. In order to protect ourselves we built, all around our camps, big fires of damp and rotten wood, that gave no flame but much smoke, and this was the cause of further trouble to us, for the whole night we did not do anything but weep from the smoke that went to our eyes, and the heat from the fires was so insufferable that we would go to the shore for rest. And when, sometimes, we were able to sleep, the Indians roused us again with blows to go and kindle the fires.

Those from further inland have another

remedy, just as bad and even worse, which is to go about with a firebrand, setting fire to the plains and timber so as to drive off the mosquitoes, and also to get lizards and similar things which they eat, to come out of the soil. In the same manner they kill deer, encircling them with fires, and they do it also to deprive the animals of pasture, compelling them to go for food where the Indians want. For never they build their abodes except where there are wood and water, and sometimes load themselves with the requisites and go in quest of deer, which are found mostly where there is neither water nor wood.

On the very day they arrive they kill deer and whatever else can be had and use all the water and wood to cook their food with and build fires against the mosquitoes. They wait for another day to get something to take along on the road, and when they leave they are so badly bitten by mosquitoes as to appear like lepers. In this manner they satisfy their hunger twice or thrice a year and at such great sacrifice as I have told. Having been with them I can say that no toil or suffering in this world comes near it.

All over this country there are a great many deer, fowl and other animals which I have before enumerated. Here also they come up with cows; I have seen them thrice and have eaten their meat. They appear to me of the size of those in Spain. Their horns are small, like those of the Moorish cattle; the hair is very long, like fine wool and like a peajacket; some are brownish and others black, and to my taste they have better and more meat than those from here. Of the small hides the Indians make blankets to cover themselves with, and of the taller ones they make shoes and targets. These cows come from the north, across the country further on, to the coast of Florida, and are found all over the land for over four hundred leagues. On this whole stretch, through the valleys by which they come, people who live there descend to subsist upon their flesh. And a great quantity of hides are met with inland.[30]

[30]In print, this is the earliest notice extant of the American Bison, or Buffalo. The Letter to the Audiencia does not mention the "cows." It

ALVAR NUNEZ CABEZA DE VACA

WHEN I had been with the Christians for six months, waiting to execute our plans, the Indians went for "tunas," at a distance of thirty leagues from there, and as we were about to flee the Indians began fighting among themselves over a woman and cuffed and struck and hurt each other, and in great rage each one took his lodge and went his own way. So we Christians had to part, and in no manner could we get together again until the year following. During that time I fared very badly, as well from lack of food as from the abuse the Indians gave me. So badly was I treated that I had to flee three times from my masters, and they all went in my pursuit ready to kill me. But God, Our Lord, in His infinite goodness, protected and saved my life.

When the time for the tunas came we found each other again on the same spot.

is probable, however, that the first report, sent to Spain by Mendoza, contained a reference to it. The *Relacion* does not reach beyond the time when they arrived at the bay, or river, of Espiritu Santo. Oviedo speaks of the cows after the book of 1542.

We had already agreed to escape and appointed a day for it, when on that very day the Indians separated us, sending each one to a different place, and I told my companions that I would wait for them at the tunas until full moon. It was the first of September and the first day of the new moon, and I told them that if at the time set they did not appear I would go on alone without them. We parted, each one going off with his Indians.

I remained with mine until the thirteenth of the moon, determined to escape to other Indians as soon as the moon would be full, and on that day there came to where I was Andrés Dorantes and Estevanico. They told me they had left Castillo with other people nearby, called *Anagados,* and how they had suffered many hardships and been lost. On the following day our Indians moved towards where Castillo was and were going to join those who kept him, making friends with them, as until then they had been at war. So we got Castillo also.

During all the time we ate tunas we felt thirsty. To allay our thirst we drank the juice of the fruit, pouring it first into a pit which we dug in the soil, and when that was full we drank to satisfaction. The Indians do it in that way, out of lack of vessels. The juice is sweet and has the color of must. There are many kinds of tunas, and some very good ones, although to me all tasted well alike, hunger never leaving me time to select, or stop to think which ones were better. Most of the people drink rain-water that collects here and there, for, as they never have a fixed abode, they know no springs nor established watering places, although there are rivers.

All over the land are vast and handsome pastures, with good grass for cattle, and it strikes me the soil would be very fertile were the country inhabited and improved by reasonable people. We saw no mountains as long as we were in this country. These Indians told us that further on there were others called *Camones,* who live nearer the coast, and that they were those who killed all the people that came in the barge of Peñalosa and Tellez. They had been so emaciated and feeble that when being killed they offered no resistance. So the Indians finished with all of them, and showed us some of their clothes and weapons and said the barge was still there stranded. This is the fifth of the missing ones. That of the Governor we already said had been swept out into the sea, the one of the purser and the monks was seen stranded on the beach and Esquivel told us of their end. Of the two in which Castillo, I and Dorantes were I have told how they sank close to the Isle of Ill-Fate.

TWO days after moving we recommended ourselves to God, Our Lord, and fled, hoping that, although it was late in the season and the fruits of the tunas were giving out, by remaining in the field we might still get over a good portion of the land. As we proceeded that day, in great fear lest the Indians would follow us, we descried smoke, and, going towards it, reached the place after sundown, where we found an Indian who, when he saw us coming, did not wait, but ran away. We sent the negro after him, and as the Indian saw him approach alone he waited. The negro told him that we were going in search of the people that had raised the smoke. He answered that the dwellings were nearby and that he would guide us, and we followed. He hurried ahead to tell of our coming. At sunset we came in sight of the lodges, and two crossbow shots before reaching them met four Indians waiting for us, and they received us well. We told them in the language of the *Mariames* that we had come to see them. They appeared to be pleased with our company and took us to their homes. They lodged Dorantes and the negro at the house of a medicine man, and me and Castillo at that of another. These Indians speak another language and are called *Avavares.* They were those who used to fetch bows to ours and barter with them, and, although of another nation and speech, they understand the idiom of those with whom we formerly were and had arrived there on that very day with their lodges. Forthwith they offered us many tunas, because they had heard of us and of how we cured and of the miracles Our Lord worked through us. And surely, even if there had been no other tokens, it was wonderful how He prepared the way for us through a country so scantily inhabited, causing us to meet people where for a long time there had been none, saving us from so many dangers, not permitting us to be killed, maintaining us through starvation and distress and moving the hearts of the people to treat us well, as we shall tell further on.

ON the night we arrived there some Indians came to Castillo complaining that their heads felt very sore and begging him for relief. As soon as he had made the sign of the cross over them and recommended them to God, at that very moment the Indians said that all the pain was gone. They went back to their abodes and brought us many tunas and a piece of venison, something we did not know any more what it was, and as the news spread that same night there came many other sick people for him to cure, and each brought a piece of venison, and so many there were that we did not know where to store the meat. We thanked God for His daily increasing mercy and kindness, and after they were all well they began to dance and celebrate and feast until sunrise of the day following.

They celebrated our coming for three days, at the end of which we asked them about the land further on, the people and the food that there might be obtained. They replied there were plenty of tunas all through that country, but that the season was over and nobody there, because all had gone to their abodes after gathering tunas; also that the country was very cold and very few hides in it. Hearing this, and as winter and cold weather were setting in, we determined to spend it with those Indians. Five days after our arrival they left to get more tunas at a place where people of a different nation and language lived, and having travelled five days, suffering greatly from hunger, as on the way there were neither tunas nor any kind of fruit, we came to a river, where we pitched our lodges.

As soon as we were settled we went out to hunt for the fruit of certain trees, which are like spring bittervetch (orobus), and as through all that country there are no trails, I lost too much time in hunting for them. The people returned without me, and starting to rejoin them that night I went astray and got lost. It pleased God to let me find a burning tree, by the fire of which I spent that very cold night, and in the morning loaded myself with wood, took two burning sticks and continued my journey. Thus I went on for five days, always with my firebrands and load of wood, so that in case the fire went out where there was no timber, as in many parts there is none, I always would have wherewith to make other torches and not be without firewood. It was my only protection against the cold, for I went as naked as a new-born child. For the night I used the following artifice:

I went to the brush in the timber near the rivers and stopped in it every evening before sunset. Then I scratched a hole in the ground and threw in it much firewood from the numerous trees. I also picked up dry wood that had fallen and built around the hole four fires crosswise, being very careful to stir them from time to time. Of the long grass that grows there I made bundles, with which I covered myself in that hole and so was protected from the night cold. But one night fire fell on the straw with which I was covered, and while I was asleep in the hole it began to burn so rapidly that, although I hurried out as quick as possible, I still have marks on my hair from this dangerous accident. During all that time I did not eat a mouthful, nor could I find anything to eat, and my feet, being bare, bled a great deal. God had mercy upon me, that in all this time there was no norther; otherwise I could not have survived.

At the end of five days I reached the shores of a river and there met my Indians. They, as well as the Christians, had given me up for dead, thinking that perhaps some snake had bitten me. They all were greatly pleased to see me, the Christians especially, and told me that thus far they had wandered about famishing, and therefore had not hunted for me, and that night they gave me of their tunas. On the next day we left and went where we found a great many of that fruit with which all appeased their hunger, and we gave many thanks to Our Lord, whose help to us never failed.

EARLY the next day many Indians came and brought five people who were paralyzed and very ill, and they came for Castillo to cure them. Every one of the patients offered him his bow and arrows, which he accepted, and by sunset he made the sign of the cross over each of the sick, recommending them to God, Our Lord, and we all prayed to Him as well as we could to restore them to health. And He, seeing there was no other way of getting those people to help us so that we might be saved from our miserable existence, had mercy upon us, and in the morning all woke up well and hearty and went away in such good health as if they never had had any ailment whatever. This caused them great admiration and moved us to thanks to Our Lord and to greater faith in His goodness and the hope that He would save us, guiding us to where we could serve Him. For myself I may say that I always had full faith in His mercy and in that He would liberate me from captivity, and always told my companions so.

When the Indians had gone and taken along those recently cured, we removed to others that were eating tunas also, called *Cultalchuches* and *Malicones,* which speak a different language, and with them were others, called *Coayos* and *Susolas,* and on another side those called *Atayos,* who were at war with the *Susolas,* and exchanging arrow shots with them every day.

Nothing was talked about in this whole country but of the wonderful cures which God, Our Lord, performed through us, and so they came from many places to be cured, and after having been with us two days some Indians of the *Susolas* begged Castillo to go and attend to a man who had been wounded, as well as to others that were sick and among whom, they said, was one on the point of death. Castillo was very timid, especially in difficult and dangerous cases, and always afraid that his sins might interfere and prevent the cures from being effective. Therefore the Indians told me to go and perform the cure. They liked me, remembering that I had relieved them while they were out gathering nuts, for which they had given us nuts and hides. This had happened at the time I was coming to join the Christians. So I had to go, and Dorantes and Estevanico went with me.

When I came close to their ranches I saw that the dying man we had been called to cure was dead, for there were many people around him weeping and his lodge was torn down, which is a sign that the owner has died. I found the Indian with eyes upturned, without pulse and with all the marks of lifelessness. At least so it seemed to me, and Dorantes said the same. I removed a mat with which he was covered, and as best I could prayed to Our Lord to restore his health, as well as that of all the others who might be in need of it, and after having made the sign of the cross and breathed on him many times they brought his bow and presented it to me, and a basket of ground tunas, and took me to many others who were suffering from vertigo. They gave me two more baskets of tunas, which I left to the Indians that had come with us. Then we returned to our quarters.

Our Indians to whom I had given the tunas remained there, and at night returned telling, that the dead man whom I attended to in their presence had resuscitated, rising from his bed, had walked about, eaten and talked to them, and that all those treated by me were well and in very good spirits. This caused great surprise and awe, and all over the land nothing else was spoken of. All who heard it came to us that we might cure them and bless their children, and when the Indians in our company (who were the *Cultalchulches*) had to return to their country, before parting they offered us all the tunas they had for their journey, not keeping a single one, and gave us flint stones as long as one and a-half palms, with which they cut and that are greatly prized among them. They begged us to remember them and pray to God to keep them always healthy, which we promised to do, and so they left, the happiest people upon earth, having given us the very best they had.

We remained with the *Avavares* Indians for eight months, according to our reckoning of the moons. During that time they came for us from many places and said that verily we were children of the sun. Until then Dorantes and the negro had not made any cures, but we found ourselves so pressed by the Indians coming from all sides, that all of us had to become medicine men. I was the most daring and reckless of all in undertaking cures. We never treated anyone that did not afterwards say he was well, and they had such confidence in our skill as to believe that none of them would die as long as we were among them.

These Indians and the ones we left behind told us a very strange tale. From their account it may have occurred fifteen or sixteen years ago. They said there wandered then about the country a man, whom they called "Bad Thing," of small stature and with a beard, although they never could see his features clearly, and whenever he would approach their dwellings their hair would stand on end and they began to tremble. In the doorway of the lodge there would then appear a firebrand. That man thereupon came in and took hold of anyone he chose, and with a sharp knife of flint, as broad as a hand and two palms in length, he cut their side, and, thrusting his hand through the gash, took out the entrails, cutting off a piece one palm long, which he threw into the fire. Afterwards he made three cuts in one of the arms, the second one at the place where people are usually bled, and twisted the arm, but reset it soon afterwards. Then he placed his hands on the wounds, and they told us that they closed at once. Many times he appeared among them while they were dancing, sometimes in the dress of a woman and again as a man, and whenever he took a notion to do it he would seize the hut or lodge, take it up into the air and come down with it again with a great crash. They also told us how, many a time, they set food before him, but he never would partake of it, and when they asked him where he came from and where he had his home, he pointed to a rent in the earth and said his house was down below.[31]

We laughed very much at those stories, making fun of them, and then, seeing our incredulity they brought to us many of those whom, they said, he had taken, and we saw the scars of his slashes in the places and as they told. We told them he was a demon and explained as best we could that if they would believe in God, Our Lord, and be Christians like ourselves, they would not have to fear that man, nor would he come and do such things unto them, and they might be sure that as long as we were in this country he would not dare to appear again. At this they were greatly pleased and lost much of their apprehension.

The same Indians told us they had seen the Asturian and Figueroa with other Indians further along on the coast, which we

[31]There is no mention of this story in Oviedo. What may be the basis for it is impossible to conjecture. It may have been a tradition, but completely misunderstood, hence misreported, by the Spaniards.

had named of the figs. All those people had no reckoning by either sun or moon, nor do they count by months and years; they judge of the seasons by the ripening of fruits, by the time when fish die and by the appearance of the stars, in all of which they are very clever and expert. While with them we were always well treated, although our food was never too plentiful, and we had to carry our own water and wood. Their dwellings and their food are like those of the others, but they are much more exposed to starvation, having neither maize nor acorns or nuts. We always went about naked like they and covered ourselves at night with deer skins.

During six of the eighteen months we were with them we suffered much from hunger, because they do not have fish either. At the end of that time the tunas began to ripen, and without their noticing it we left and went to other Indians further ahead, called *Maliacones,* at a distance of one day's travel. Three days after I and the negro reached there I sent him back to get Castillo and Dorantes, and after they rejoined me we all departed in company of the Indians, who went to eat a small fruit of some trees. On this fruit they subsist for ten or twelve days until the tunas are fully ripe. There they joined other Indians called *Arbadaos,* whom we found to be so sick, emaciated and swollen that we were greatly astonished. The Indians with whom we had come went back on the same trail, and we told them that we wished to remain with the others, at which they showed grief. So we remained with the others in the field near their dwellings.

When the Indians saw us they clustered together, after having talked among themselves, and each one of them took the one of us whom he claimed by the hand and they led us to their homes. While with those we suffered more from hunger than among any of the others. In the course of a whole day we did not eat more than two handfuls of the fruit, which was green and contained so much milky juice that our mouths were burnt by it. As water was very scarce, whoever ate of them became very thirsty. And we finally grew so hungry that we purchased two dogs, in exchange for nets and other things, and a hide with which I used to cover myself. I have said already that through all that country we went naked, and not being accustomed to it, like snakes we shed our skin twice a year. Exposure to the sun and air covered our chests and backs with big sores that made it very painful to carry the big and heavy loads, the ropes of which cut into the flesh of our arms.

The country is so rough and overgrown that often after we had gathered firewood in the timber and dragged it out, we would bleed freely from the thorns and spines which cut and slashed us wherever they touched. Sometimes it happened that I was unable to carry or drag out the firewood after I had gathered it with much loss of blood. In all that trouble my only relief or consolation was to remember the passion of our Saviour, Jesus Christ, and the blood He shed for me, and to ponder how much greater His sufferings had been from the thorns, than those I was then enduring. I made a contract with the Indians to make combs, arrows, bows and nets for them.

Also we made matting of which their lodges are constructed and of which they are in very great need, for, although they know how to make it, they do not like to do any work, in order to be able to go in quest of food. Whenever they work they suffer greatly from hunger.

Again, they would make me scrape skins and tan them, and the greatest luxury I enjoyed was on the day they would give me a skin to scrape, because I scraped it very deep in order to eat the parings, which would last me two or three days. It also happened to us, while being with these Indians and those before mentioned, that we would eat a piece of meat which they gave us, raw, because if we broiled it the first Indian coming along would snatch and eat it; it seemed useless to take any pains, in view of what we might expect; neither were we particular to go to any trouble in order to have it broiled and might just as well eat it raw. Such was the life we led there, and even that scanty maintenance we had to earn through the objects made by our own hands for barter.

ALVAR NUNEZ CABEZA DE VACA

AFTER we had eaten the dogs it seemed to us that we had enough strength to go further on, so we commended ourselves to the guidance of God, Our Lord, took leave of these Indians, and they put us on the track of others of their language who were nearby. While on our way it began to rain and rained the whole day. We lost the trail and found ourselves in a big forest, where we gathered plenty of leaves of tunas which we roasted that same night in an oven made by ourselves, and so much heat did we give them that in the morning they were fit to be eaten. After eating them we recommended ourselves to God again, and left, and struck the trail we had lost.

Issuing from the timber, we met other Indian dwellings, where we saw two women and some boys, who were so frightened at the sight of us that they fled to the forest to call the men that were in the woods. When these came they hid behind trees to peep at us. We called them and they approached in great fear. After we addressed them they told us they were very hungry and that nearby were many of their own lodges, and they would take us to them. So that night we reached a site where there were fifty dwellings, and the people were stupefied at seeing us and showed much fear. After they had recovered from their astonishment they approached and put their hands to our faces and bodies and afterwards to their faces and bodies also. We stayed there that night, and in the morning they brought their sick people, begging us to cross them, and gave us of what they had to eat, which were leaves of tunas and green tunas baked.

For the sake of this good treatment, giving us all they had, content with being without anything for our sake, we remained with them several days, and during that time others came from further on. When those were about to leave we told the first ones that we intended to accompany them. This made them very sad, and they begged us on their knees not to go. But we went and left them in tears at our departure, as it pained them greatly.

FROM the Island of Ill-Fate on, all the Indians whom we met as far as to here have the custom of not cohabiting with their wives when these are pregnant, and until the child is two years old.[32]

Children are nursed to the age of twelve years, when they are old enough to gather their own food. We asked them why they brought their children up in that way and they replied, it was owing to the great scarcity of food all over that country, since it was common (as we saw) to be without it two or three days, and even four, and for that reason they nursed the little ones so long to preserve them from perishing through hunger. And even if they should survive, they would be very delicate and weak. When one falls sick he is left to die in the field unless he be somebody's child. Other invalids, if unable to travel, are abandoned; but a son or brother is taken along.

There is also a custom for husbands to

[32]Not in Oviedo. He mentions it, however (on p. 617), as stated by Cabeza de Vaca in his book. The same in regard to the following sentences.

leave their wives if they do not agree, and to remarry whom they please; this applies to the young men, but after they have had children they stay with their women and do not leave them.

When, in any village, they quarrel among themselves, they strike and beat each other until worn out, and only then do they separate. Sometimes their women step in and separate them, but men never interfere in these brawls. Nor do they ever use bow and arrow, and after they have fought and settled the question, they take their lodges and women and go out into the field to live apart from the others till their anger is over, and when they are no longer angry and their resentment has passed away they return to the village and are as friendly again as if nothing had happened. There is no need of mediation. When the quarrel is between unmarried people they go to some of the neighbors, who, even if they be enemies, will receive them well, with great festivities and gifts of what they have, so that, when pacified, they return to their village wealthy.

They all are warriors and so astute in guarding themselves from an enemy as if trained in continuous wars and in Italy. When in places where their enemies can offend them, they set their lodges on the edge of the roughest and densest timber and dig a trench close to it in which they sleep. The men at arms are hidden by brushwood and have their loopholes, and are so well covered and concealed that even at close range they cannot be seen.

To the densest part of the forest they open a very narrow trail and there arrange a sleeping place for their women and children. As night sets in they build fires in the lodges, so that if there should be spies about, these would think the people to sleep there. And before sunrise they light the same fires again. Now, ditches, without being seen or discovered.

In case there are no forests wherein they can hide thus and prepare their ambushes, they settle on the plain wherever it appears most appropriate, surrounding the place with trenches protected by brushwood. In these they open loopholes through which they can reach the enemy with arrows, and those parapets they build for the night. While I was with the *Aguenes* and these not on their guard, their enemies surprised them at midnight, killing three and wounding a number, so that they fled from their houses to the forest. As soon, however, as they noticed that the others had gone they went back, picked up all the arrows the others had spent and left and followed them as stealthily as possible. That same night they reached the others' dwellings unnoticed, and at sunrise attacked, killing five, besides wounding a great many. The rest made their escape, leaving homes and bows behind, with all their other belongings.

A short time after this the women of those calling themselves *Guevenes* came, held a parley and made them friends again, but sometimes women are also the cause of war. All those people when they have personal questions and are not of one family, kill each other in a treacherous way and deal most cruelly with one another.

ALVAR NUNEZ CABEZA DE VACA

THOSE Indians are the readiest people with their weapons of all I have seen in the world, for when they suspect the approach of an enemy they lie awake all night with their bows within reach and a dozen of arrows, and before one goes to sleep he tries his bow, and should the string not be to his liking he arranges it until it suits him. Often they crawl out of their dwellings so as not to be seen and look and spy in every direction after danger, and if they detect anything, in less than no time are they all out in the field with their bows and arrows. Thus they remain until daybreak, running hither and thither whenever they see danger or suspect their enemies might approach. When day comes they unstring their bows until they go hunting.

The strings of their bows are made of deer sinews. They fight in a crouching posture, and while shooting at each other talk and dart from one side to the other to dodge the arrows of the foe. In this way they receive little damage from our crossbows and muskets. On the contrary, the Indians laugh at those weapons, because they are not dangerous to them on the plains over which they roam. They are only good in narrows and in swamps.

Horses are what the Indians dread most, and by means of which they will be overcome.

Whoever has to fight Indians must take great care not to let them think he is disheartened or that he covets what they own; in war they must be treated very harshly, for should they notice either fear or greed, they are the people who know how to abide their time for revenge and to take courage from the fears of their enemy. After spending all their arrows, they part, going each their own way, and without attempting pursuit, although one side might have more men than the other; such is their custom.

Many times they are shot through and through with arrows, but do not die from the wounds as long as the bowels or heart are not touched; on the contrary, they recover quickly. Their eyesight, hearing and senses in general are better, I believe, than those of any other men upon earth. They can stand, and have to stand, much hunger, thirst and cold, being more accustomed and used to it than others. This I wished to state here, since, besides that all men are curious to know the habits and devices of others, such as might come in contact with those people should be informed of their customs and deeds, which will be of no small profit to them.

I ALSO do wish to tell of the nations and languages met with from the Island of Ill-Fate to the last ones, the *Cuchendados.* On the Island of Ill-Fate two languages are spoken, the ones they call *Capoques,* the others *Han.* On the mainland, facing the island, are others, called of *Charruco,* who take their name from the woods in which they live. Further on, along the seashore, are others, who call themselves *Deguenes,* and in front of them others named those of *Mendica.* Further on, on the coast, are the *Quevenes,* in front further inland the *Mariames,* and following the coast we come to the *Guaycones,* and in front of them inland the *Yeguaces.* After those come the *Atayos,* and behind them others, called *Decubadaos,* of whom there are a great many further on in this direction. On the coast live the *Quitoles,* and in front of them, inland, the *Chauauares.* These are joined by the *Maliacones* and the *Cultalchulches* and others called *Susolas* and *Comos,* ahead on the coast are the *Camolas,* and further on those whom we call the people of the figs.[33]

All those people have homes and villages and speak different languages. Among them is a language wherein they call men *mira aca, arraca,* and dogs *xó.*

In this whole country they make themselves drunk by a certain smoke for which they give all they have. They also drink something which they extract from leaves of

[33]Oviedo gives no names of tribes. How far they may be reliable is extremely problematic. In the first place, it is very doubtful if Cabeza de Vaca understood as much of the language of the different tribes as he insinuates; and next, even if they are really names of distinct tribes or bands, we cannot determine whether they were those which they gave to themselves or those given to them by others, which is always a great difference.

trees, like unto water-oak, toasting them on the fire in a vessel like a low-necked bottle. When the leaves are toasted they fill the vessel with water and hold it over the fire so long until it has thrice boiled; then they pour the liquid into a bowl made of a gourd cut in twain. As soon as there is much foam on it they drink it as hot as they can stand, and from the time they take it out of the first vessel until they drink they shout, "Who wants to drink?" When the women hear this they stand still at once, and although they carry a very heavy load do not dare to move. Should one of them stir, she is dishonored and beaten. In a great rage they spill the liquid they have prepared and spit out what they drank, easily and without pain. The reason for this custom, they say, is that when they want to drink that water and the women stir from the spot where they first hear the shouts, an evil substance gets into the liquid that penetrates their bodies, causing them to die before long. All the time the water boils the vessel must be kept covered. Should it be uncovered while a woman comes along they pour it out and do not drink of it. It is yellow and they drink it for three days without partaking of any food, each consuming an arroba and a half every day.

When the women are ill they only seek food for themselves, because nobody else eats of what they bring.[34]

During the time I was among them I saw something very repulsive, namely, a man married to another. Such are impotent and womanish beings, who dress like women and perform the office of women, but use the bow and carry big loads. Among these Indians we saw many of them; they are more robust than the other men, taller, and can bear heavy burthens.

After parting from those we had left in tears, we went with the others to their homes and were very well received. They brought us their children to touch, and gave us much mezquite-meal. This mezquiquez[36] is a fruit

[34]Not in Letter to Audiencia, but Oviedo mentions it as contained in Cabeza de Vaca.

[36]The well-known Mesquite tree. The report in Oviedo does not make mention of it, but in Chapter VII, of Book XXXV, Vol. III, p. 617, Oviedo copies almost literally this passage relative to Mesquite.

which, while on the tree, is very bitter and like the carob bean. It is eaten with earth and then becomes sweet and very palatable. The way they prepare it is to dig a hole in the ground, of the depth it suits them, and after the fruit is put in that hole, with a piece of wood, the thickness of a leg and one and a half fathoms long they pound it to a meal, and to the earth that mixes with it in the hole they add several handfuls and pound again for a while. After that they empty it into a vessel, like a small, round basket, and pour in enough water to cover it fully, so that there is water on top. Then the one who has done the pounding tastes it, and if it appears to him not sweet enough he calls for more earth to add, and this he does until it suits his taste. Then all squat around and every one reaches out with his hand and takes as much as he can. The seeds and peelings they set apart on hides, and the one who has done the pounding throws them back into the vessel, pouring water over them again. They squeeze out the juice and water, and the husks and seeds they again put on hides, repeating the operation three or four times at every pounding. Those who take part in that banquet, which is for them a great occasion, get very big bellies from the earth and water they swallow.

Now, of this, the Indians made a great feast in our behalf, and danced and celebrated all the time we were with them. And at night six Indians, to each one of us, kept watch at the entrance to the lodge we slept in, without allowing anybody to enter before sunrise.

When we were about to leave some women happened to come, that belonged to Indians living further on, and, informing ourselves where their abodes were, we left, although the Indians entreated us to remain a day longer, since the place we wanted to go to was very far away, and there was no trail to it. They showed us how the women who had just arrived were tired, but that if we would let them rest until the next day, they then would accompany and guide us. We left, nevertheless, and soon the women followed with others of the village.

There being no trails in that country, we

soon lost our way. At the end of four leagues we reached a spring, and there met the women who had followed us, and who told us of all they had gone through until they fell in with us again. We went on, taking them along as guides.

In the afternoon we crossed a big river, the water being more than waist-deep. It may have been as wide as the one of Sevilla, and had a swift current. At sunset we reached a hundred Indian huts and, as we approached, the people came out to receive us, shouting frightfully, and slapping their thighs. They carried perforated gourds filled with pebbles, which are ceremonial objects of great importance. They only use them at dances, or as medicine, to cure, and nobody dares touch them but themselves. They claim that those gourds have healing virtues, and that they come from Heaven, not being found in that country; nor do they know where they come from, except that the rivers carry them down when they rise and overflow the land.

So great was their excitement and eagerness to touch us that, every one wanting to be first, they nearly squeezed us to death, and, without suffering our feet to touch the ground, carried us to their abodes. So many crowded down upon us that we took refuge in the lodges they had prepared for our accommodation, and in no manner consented to be feasted by them on that night.

The whole night they spent in celebration and dancing,[37] and the next morning they brought us every living soul of that village to be touched by us and to have the cross made over them, as with the others. Then they gave to the women of the other village who had come with their own a great many arrows. The next day we went on, and all the people of that village with us, and when

[37]It is perhaps not amiss to call attention here to the fact that an Indian dance is much more of a religious performance than a mere rejoicing. This Cabeza de Vaca, of course, did not, and could not, know. The dances may just as well have been, in part at least, conjurations, either to implore the spirits to intercede for them with the mysterious strangers, or to protect the Indians from any evil the newcomers might intend to inflict, by rendering them harmless. Of course, the further on the Spaniards went, and the better it became known that their actions were beneficial, the more these ceremonies had to assume the character of intercession only, coupled with thanks for the coming (or sending) of such powerfully beneficial beings.

we came to other Indians were as well received as anywhere in the past; they also gave us of what they had and the deer they had killed during the day. Among these we saw a new custom. Those who were with us took away from those people who came to get cured their bows and arrows, their shoes and beads, if they wore any, and placed them before us to induce us to cure the sick. As soon as these had been treated they went away contented and saying they felt well.

So we left there also, going to others, by whom we were also very well received, and they brought us their sick, who, after we had made the sign of the cross over them, would say they were healed, and he who did not get well still believed we might cure him. And at what the others whom we had treated told they rejoiced and danced so much as not to let us sleep.

After we left those we went to many other lodges, but thence on there prevailed a new custom. While we were received very well everywhere, those who came with us would treat those who received us badly, taking away their belongings and plundering their homes, without leaving them anything. It grieved us very much to see how those who were so good to us were abused. Besides, we dreaded lest this behavior might cause trouble and strife. But as we could not venture to interfere or punish the transgressors, we had to wait until we might have more authority over them. Furthermore, the sufferers themselves, noticing how we felt, comforted us by saying we should not worry; that they were so happy at seeing us as to gladly lose their own, considering it to be well employed, and besides, that further on they would repay themselves from other Indians who were very rich. On that whole journey we were much worried by the number of people following us. We could not escape them, although we tried, because they were so anxious to touch us, and so obtrusive that in three hours we could not get through with them.

The following day they brought us all the people of the village; most of them had one eye clouded, while others were totally blind from the same cause, at which we were amazed. They are well built, of very good physique, and whiter than any we had met until then. There we began to see mountains, and it seemed as if they swept down from the direction of the North Sea, and so, from what the Indians told us, we believe they are fifteen leagues from the ocean.[38]

From there we went with the Indians towards the mountains aforesaid, and they took us to some of their relatives. They did not want to lead us anywhere but to their own people, so as to prevent their enemies having any share in the great boon which,

[38]Elsewhere I have observed that the terms, north, or south, sea, indicate, not the north and south respectively, but east and west; the north sea being the Atlantic and the south sea the Pacific. Hence the mountains here mentioned extended, at least approximately, from east to west. As will be seen further on, the slopes of these mountains were covered with "iron slags," indicating volcanic rock. This may lead to the identification of the chain of mountains described by Cabeza de Vaca.

as they fancied, it was to see us. And as soon as we would arrive those that went with us would sack the houses of the others; but as these knew of the custom before our coming, they hid some of their chattels, and, after receiving us with much rejoicing, they took out the things which they had concealed and presented them to us. These were beads and ochre, and several little bags of silver.[39] We, following the custom, turned the gifts immediately over to the Indians who had come in our company, and after they had given these presents they began their dances and celebrations, and sent for others from another village near by to come and look at us. In the afternoon they all came, and brought us beads, bows, and other little things, which we also distributed.

The next day, as we were going to leave, they all wanted to take us to others of their

[39]In place of "silver," the edition of 1555 has "*margarita*," which may stand for mica, or else foliated gypsum. Mica is more likely. Oviedo (*ut supra*) says: "This last relation [the one of 1542] says the Indians gave to those Christians [Cabeza de Vaca and his companions] some little bags with silver, which is a mistake of the printer, who should have put, little bags with *margarita* (mica), and not 'with silver.' "

friends, who dwelt on a spur of the mountains. They said there were a great many lodges, and people who would give us much, but, as it was out of our way, we did not want to go there, and continued on the plain, though near the mountains, thinking them to be not far from the coast. All the people there are very bad, and we preferred to cross the country, as further inland they were better inclined, and treated us better. We also felt sure to find the country more thickly settled and with more resources. Finally, we did it because, in crossing the country, we would see much more of its particulars, so that, in case God our Lord should be pleased to spare one of us and take him back to a land of Christians, he might give an account of it.

When the Indians saw we were determined not to go whither they wanted, they said that nobody lived where we intended to go, neither were there tunas nor any other food, and they entreated us to tarry one day longer with them, to which we consented. Two Indians were sent out to look for people on our proposed route.

The next day we departed, taking many of them along, the women carrying water, and so great had become our authority that none dared to drink without our permission. After going two leagues we met the men sent out in search of people, but who had not found any. At this the Indians seemed to show grief, and again begged us to take the way of the mountains, but we persisted, and, seeing this, they took mournful leave of us and turned back down the river to their homes, while we proceeded along the stream upwards.

Soon we met two women carrying loads. As they descried us they stood still, put down their loads, and brought us of what these contained, which was cornmeal, and told us that higher up on the river we would meet with dwellings, plenty of tunas, and of that same meat. We left them, as they were going to those from whom we had just taken leave, and walked on until at sunset we reached a village of about twenty lodges, where they received us with tears and deep sorrow. They already knew that, wherever we arrived, the people would be robbed and plundered by those in our company. But, seeing us alone, they lost their fear, and gave us tunas, though nothing else. We stayed there over night.

At daybreak the same Indians we had left the day before surprised the lodges, and, as the people were unprepared, in fancied security, and had neither time nor place to hide anything, they were stripped of all their chattels, at which they wept bitterly. In consolation, the robbers told them that we were children of the sun, and had the power to cure or kill, and other lies, bigger even than those which they invent to suit their purposes. They also enjoined them to treat us with great reverence, and be careful not to arouse our wrath; to give us all they had and guide us to where there were many people, and that wherever we should come to they should steal and rob everything the others had, such being the custom.

After giving these instructions, and teaching the people how to behave, they returned, and left us with these Indians, who, mindful of what the others had said, began to treat us with the same respect and awe, and we travelled in their company for three days. They took us to where there were many Indians, and went ahead to tell them of our coming, repeating what they had heard and adding much more to it, for all these Indians are great gossipers and liars, particularly when they think it to be to their benefit. As we neared the lodges all the inmates came out to receive us, with much rejoicing and display, and, among other things, two of their medicine-men gave us two gourds. Thence onward we carried gourds, which added greatly to our authority, since they hold these ceremonial objects very high.[40] Our companions sacked the dwellings, but as there were many and they only few in number, they could not carry away all they took, so that more than half was left to waste. Thence we turned inland for more than fifty leagues, following the slopes of the mountains, and at the end of them met forty dwellings.

There, among other things which they gave us, Andrés Dorantes got a big rattle

[40]The well-known rattles of the medicine-men, also used largely in dances.

of copper, large, on which was represented a face, and which they held in great esteem. They said it had been obtained from some of their neighbors. Upon asking these whence it had come, they claimed to have brought it from the north, where there was much of it and highly prized. We understood that, wherever it might have come from, there must be foundries, and that metal was cast in molds.[41] Leaving on the next day, we crossed a mountain seven leagues long, the stones of which were iron slags. At night we came to many dwellings, situated on the banks of a very beautiful river.

The inmates of these abodes came to receive us halfways, with their children on their backs. They gave us a number of pouches with silver[42] and powdered antimony (or lead),[43] with which they paint

[41]This recalls the copper plate on the breast of a chief Quivira. (Compare the "Journey of Coronado," in this series.) That Indian did as little know the origin of the ornament he was wearing (although Nebraska lies considerably nearer the deposits of native copper than Texas) than the Indians of Cabeza de Vaca. From the (of course, fancied) belief in the existence of foundries, we may infer that the rattle was cast.

[42]Should be mica (*margarita*).

[43]This may have been war-paint, both lead and antimony procuring a dark-bluish hue on the

their faces, and many beads and robes of cow-skins, and loaded those who came with us with all their chattels. These people ate tunas and pine-nuts; there are in that country small trees of the sweet pine,[44] the cones of which are like small eggs, but the nuts are better than those of Castilla, because the husks are thin. When still green they grind them and make balls that are eaten. When dried they grind the nuts with the husks, and eat them as meal. And those who received us, as soon as they had touched our bodies, returned to their houses on a run, then came again, and never stopped running back and forth. In this way they brought us a great many things for our journey.

Here they brought to me a man who, they told, a long time ago had been shot through the left side of the back with an arrow, the head of which stuck close to his heart. He said it gave him much pain, and that on this

skin. In New Mexico a manganese ore is used for war-paint.

[44]*Pinus edulis,* the well-known Piñon tree with its edible nuts. If the statement of Cabeza de Vaca, "in that country," means the place where he was *then,* it must have been somewhere within the triangle formed by the Rio Grande and the Pecos rivers, where the nut pine exists to-day.

account he was sick. I touched the region of the body and felt the arrowhead, and that it had pierced the cartilage. So, with a knife, I cut open the breast as far as the place. The arrow point had gotten athwart, and was very difficult to remove. By cutting deeper, and inserting the point of the knife, with great difficulty I got it out; it was very long. Then, with a deer-bone, according to my knowledge of surgery, I made two stitches. After I had extracted the arrow they begged me for it, and I gave it to them. The whole village came back to look at it, and they sent it further inland that the people there might see it also.

On account of this cure they made many dances and festivities, as is their custom. The next day I cut the stitches, and the Indian was well. The cut I had made only showed a scar like a line in the palm of the hand, and he said that he felt not the least pain.

Now, this cure gave us such fame among them all over the country as they were capable of conceiving and respecting. We showed them our rattle, and they told us that where it had come from there were a great many sheets of the same (metal) buried,[45] that it was a thing they valued highly, and that there were fixed abodes at the place. We believe it to be near the South Sea, for we always heard that sea was richer (in metal) than the one of the north.

After leaving these people we travelled among so many different tribes and languages that nobody's memory can recall them all, and always they robbed each other; but those who lost and those who gained were equally content. The number of our companions became so large that we could no longer control them.

Going through these valleys each Indian carried a club three palms in length. They all moved in a front, and whenever a hare (of which there are many) jumped up they closed in upon the game, and rained such blows upon it that it was amazing to see. Thus they drove the hare from one to the other, and, to my fancy, it was the most agreeable chase that could be thought of, for many a time they would come right to

[45]This seems an allusion to native copper.

one's hands; and when at night we camped they had given us so many that each one of us had eight or ten loads.[46] Those of the Indians who carried bows would not take part, but went to the mountains after deer, and when at night they came back it was with five or six deer for each one of us, with birds, quails, and other game; in short, all those people could kill they set before us, without ever daring to touch anything, even if dying of hunger, unless we blessed it first. Such was their custom from the time they joined us.

The women brought many mats, with which they built us houses, one for each of us and those attached to him. After this we would order them to broil all the game, and they did it quickly in ovens built by them for the purpose. We partook of everything a little, giving the rest to the principal man among those who had come with us for distribution among all. Every one then came with the share he had received for us to breathe on it and bless it, without which they

[46]This recalls the ceremonial rabbit-hunt of the Pueblo Indians of New Mexico.

left it untouched. Often we had with us three to four thousand persons. And it was very tiresome to have to breathe on and make the sign of the cross over every morsel they ate or drank. For many other things which they wanted to do they would come to ask our permission, so that it is easy to realize how greatly we were bothered. The women brought us tunas, spiders, worms, and whatever else they could find, for they would rather starve than partake of anything that had not first passed through our hands.

While travelling with those, we crossed a big river coming from the north and, traversing about thirty leagues of plains, met a number of people that came from afar to meet us on the trail, who treated us like the foregoing ones.

Thence on there was a change in the manner of reception, insofar as those who would meet us on the trail with gifts were no longer robbed by the Indians of our company, but after we had entered their homes they tendered us all they possessed, and the dwellings also. We turned over everything to the principals for distribution. Invariably those who had been deprived of their belongings would follow us, in order to repair their losses, so that our retinue became very large. They would tell them to be careful and not conceal anything of what they owned, as it could not be done without our knowledge, and then we would cause their death. So much did they frighten them that on the first few days after joining us they would be trembling all the time, and would not dare to speak or lift their eyes to Heaven.

Those guided us for more than fifty leagues through a desert of very rugged mountains, and so arid that there was no game. Consequently we suffered much from lack of food, and finally forded a very big river, with its water reaching to our chest. Thence on many of our people began to show the effects of the hunger and hardships they had undergone in those mountains, which were extremely barren and tiresome to travel.

The same Indians led us to a plain beyond the chain of mountains, where people came to meet us from a long distance. By those we were treated in the same manner as before, and they made so many presents to the Indians who came with us that, unable to carry all, they left half of it. We told the givers to take it back, so as not to have it lost, but they refused, saying it was not their custom to take back what they had once offered, and so it was left to waste. We told these people our route was towards sunset, and they replied that in that direction people lived very far away. So we ordered them to send there and inform the inhabitants that we were coming and how. From this they begged to be excused, because the others were their enemies, and they did not want us to go to them. Yet they did not venture to disobey in the end, and sent two women, one of their own and the other a captive. They selected women because these can trade everywhere, even if there be war.

We followed the women to a place where it had been agreed we should wait for them. After five days they had not yet returned, and the Indians explained that it might be because they had not found anybody. So we told them to take us north, and they repeated that there were no people, except very far away, and neither food nor water. Nevertheless we insisted, saying that we wanted to go there, and they still excused themselves as best they could, until at last we became angry.

One night I went away to sleep out in the field apart from them; but they soon came to where I was, and remained awake all night in great alarm, talking to me, saying how frightened they were. They entreated us not to be angry any longer, because, even if it was their death, they would take us where we chose. We feigned to be angry still, so as to keep them in suspense, and then a singular thing happened.

On that same day many fell sick, and on the next day eight of them died! All over the country, where it was known, they became so afraid that it seemed as if the mere sight of us would kill them. They besought us not to be angry nor to procure the death of any more of their number, for they were convinced that we killed them by merely thinking of it. In truth, we were very much concerned about it, for, seeing the great mortality, we dreaded that all of them might die or forsake us in their terror, while those further on, upon learning of it, would get out of our way hereafter. We prayed to God our Lord to assist us, and the sick began to get well. Then we saw something that astonished us very much, and it was that, while the parents, brothers and wives of the dead had shown deep grief at their illness, from the moment they died the survivors made no demonstration whatsoever, and showed not the slightest feeling; nor did they dare to go near the bodies until we ordered their burial.

In more than fifteen days that we remained with them we never saw them talk together, neither did we see a child that laughed or cried. One child, who had begun to cry, was carried off some distance, and with some very sharp mice-teeth they scratched it from the shoulders down to nearly the legs. Angered by this act of cruelty, I took them to task for it, and they said it was done to punish the child for having wept in my presence. Their apprehensions caused the others that came to see us to give us what they had, since they knew that we did not take anything for ourselves, but left it all to the Indians.

Those were the most docile people we met in the country, of the best complexion, and on the whole well built.

The sick being on the way of recovery, when we had been there already three days, the women whom we had sent out returned, saying that they had met very few people, nearly all having gone after the cows, as it was the season. So we ordered those who had been sick to remain, and those who were well to accompany us, and that, two days' travel from there, the same women should go with us and get people to come to meet us on the trail for our reception.

The next morning all those who were strong enough came along, and at the end of three journeys we halted. Alonso del Castillo and Estevanico, the negro, left with the women as guides, and the woman who was a captive took them to a river that flows between mountains,[47] where there was a village, in which her father lived, and these were the first abodes we saw that were like unto real houses. Castillo and Estevanico went to these and, after holding parley with the Indians, at the end of three days Castillo returned to where he had left us, bringing with him five or six of the Indians. He told how he had found permanent houses, inhabited, the people of which ate beans and squashes,[48] and that he had also seen maize.

Of all things upon earth this caused us the greatest pleasure, and we gave endless thanks to our Lord for this news. Castillo also said that the negro was coming to meet us on the way, near by, with all the people of the houses. For that reason we started, and after going a league and a half met the negro and the people that came to receive

[47]This being the last important stream met by the wanderers before they reached the Pacific states of Mexico, it may be permitted to inquire whether it was not perhaps the Rio Grande, in which case the stream previously mentioned, and along which the "cows" were roaming, was the Pecos.

[48]The originals have *"melones,"* but I have no doubt that a species of squash is meant.

us, who gave us beans and many squashes to eat, gourds to carry water in, robes of cowhide, and other things. As those people and the Indians of our company were enemies, and did not understand each other, we took leave of the latter, leaving them all that had been given to us, while we went on with the former and, six leagues beyond, when night was already approaching, reached their houses, where they received us with great ceremonies. Here we remained one day, and left on the next, taking them with us to other permanent houses, where they subsisted on the same food also, and thence on we found a new custom.

The people who heard of our approach did not, as before, come out to meet us on the way, but we found them at their homes, and they had other houses ready for us. They were all seated with their faces turned to the wall, the heads bowed and the hair pulled over the eyes. Their belongings had been gathered in a heap in the middle of the floor, and thence on they began to give us many robes of skins. There was nothing they would not give us. They are the best formed people we have seen, the liveliest and most capable; who best understood us and answered our questions. We called them "of the cows," because most of the cows die near there,[49] and because for more than fifty leagues up that stream they go to kill many of them. Those people go completely naked, after the manner of the first we met. The women are covered with deerskins, also some men, especially the old ones, who are of no use any more in war.

The country is well settled. We asked them why they did not raise maize, and they replied that they were afraid of losing the crops, since for two successive years it had not rained, and the seasons were so dry that the moles had eaten the corn, so that they did not dare to plant any more until it should have rained very hard. And they also begged us to ask Heaven for rain, which we promised to do. We also wanted to know from where they brought their maize, and they said it came from where the sun sets, and that it was found all over that

[49]Which is to say, that they are hunted and killed in that vicinity.

country, and the shortest way to it was in that direction. We asked them to tell us how to go, as they did not want to go themselves, to tell us about the way.

They said we should travel up the river towards the north, on which trail for seventeen days we would not find a thing to eat, except a fruit called *chacan,* which they grind between stones; but even then it cannot be eaten, being so coarse and dry; and so it was, for they showed it to us and we could not eat it. But they also said that, going upstream, we would always travel among people who were their enemies, although speaking the same language, and who could give us no food, but would receive us very willingly, and give us many cotton blankets, hides and other things; but that it seemed to them that we ought not to take that road.

In doubt as to what should be done, and which was the best and most advantageous road to take, we remained with them for two days. They gave us beans, squashes,[50] and calabashes. Their way of cooking them

[50]Original has "*melones.*"

is so new and strange that I felt like describing it here, in order to show how different and queer are the devices and industries of human beings. They have no pots. In order to cook their food they fill a middle-sized gourd with water, and place into a fire such stones as easily become heated, and when they are hot to scorch they take them out with wooden tongs, thrusting them into the water of the gourd, until it boils. As soon as it boils they put into it what they want to cook, always taking out the stones as they cool off and throwing in hot ones to keep the water steadily boiling. This is their way of cooking.

After two days were past we determined to go in search of maize, and not to follow the road to the cows, since the latter carried us to the north, which meant a very great circuit, as we held it always certain that by going towards sunset we should reach the goal of our wishes.[51]

[51]By following the Rio Grande from the mouth of the Pecos, they indeed would have travelled almost due west for about a hundred and fifty

So we went on our way and traversed the whole country to the South Sea, and our resolution was not shaken by the fear of great starvation, which the Indians said we should suffer (and indeed suffered) during the first seventeen days of travel. All along the river, and in the course of these seventeen days we received plenty of cowhides, and did not eat of their famous fruit (*chacan*), but our food consisted (for each day) of a handful of deer-tallow, which for that purpose we always sought to keep, and so endured these seventeen days, at the end of which we crossed the river and marched for seventeen days more. At sunset, on a plain between very high mountains, we met people who, for one-third of the year, eat but powdered straw, and as we went by just at that time, had to eat it also, until, at the end of that journey we found some permanent houses, with plenty of harvested maize, of which and of its meal they gave us great quantities, also squashes and beans, and blankets of cotton, with all of which

miles, and thence northwest for about eighty miles more, by air line; whereas, by ascending the Pecos they had to go due north.

we loaded those who had conducted us thither, so that they went home the most contented people upon earth. We gave God our Lord many thanks for having taken us where there was plenty to eat.

Among the houses there were several made of earth, and others of cane matting; and from here we travelled more than a hundred leagues, always meeting permanent houses and a great stock of maize and beans, and they gave us many deer (-hides?) and blankets of cotton better than those of New Spain. They also gave us plenty of beads made out of the coral found in the South Sea; many good turquoises, which they get from the north; they finally gave us all they had; and Dorantes they presented with five emeralds, shaped as arrow-points, which arrows they use in their feasts and dances.[52] As they appeared to be of very good quality, I asked whence they got them from, and

[52]The "emeralds" are not mentioned in the report published by Oviedo, but Oviedo himself refers to them (p. 618) from the 1542 edition. It is not unlikely they were malachites. I saw, in possession of a prominent medicine-man from the Pueblo of San Juan, in New Mexico, a plate of malachite shaped like a large, blunt knife, which he said had come from Chihuahua. It was, of

they said it was from some very high mountains toward the north, where they traded for them with feather-bushes and parrot-plumes, and they said also that there were villages with many people and very big houses.

Among those people we found the women better treated than in any other part of the Indies as far as we have seen. They wear skirts of cotton that reach as far as the knee, and over them half-sleeves of scraped deer-skin, with strips that hang down to the ground, and which they clean with certain roots, that clean very well and thus keep them tidy. The shirts are open in front and tied with strings; they wear shoes.

All those people came to us that we might touch and cross them; and they were so obtrusive as to make it difficult to endure since all, sick and healthy, wanted to be crossed. It happened frequently that women of our company would give birth to children and

course, not transparent, but had a fine emerald hue, with dendrites. In South America (Peru and Bolivia) among the common people emeralds having a so-called "garden"—that is, imperfectly transparent specimens—are highly prized, provided their color is deep green.

forthwith bring them to have the sign of the cross made over them and the babes be touched by us. They always accompanied us until we were again in the care of others, and all those people believed that we came from Heaven. What they do not understand or is new to them they are wont to say it comes from above.

While travelling with these we used to go the whole day without food, until night, and then we would eat so little that the Indians were amazed. They never saw us tired, because we were, in reality, so inured to hardships as not to feel them any more. We exercised great authority over them, and carried ourselves with much gravity, and, in order to maintain it, spoke very little to them. It was the negro who talked to them all the time; he inquired about the road we should follow, the villages—in short, about everything we wished to know. We came across a great variety and number of languages, and God our Lord favored us with a knowledge of all, because they always could understand us and we understood them, so that when we asked they would answer by signs, as if they spoke our tongue and we theirs; for, although we spoke six languages,[53] not everywhere could we use them, since we found more than a thousand different ones. In that part of the country those who were at war would at once make peace and become friendly to each other, in order to meet us and bring us all they possessed; and thus we left the whole country at peace.

We told them, by signs which they understood, that in Heaven there was a man called God, by us, who had created Heaven and earth, and whom we worshipped as our Lord; that we did as he ordered us to do, all good things coming from his hand, and that if they were to do the same they would become very happy; and so well were they inclined that, had there been a language in which we could have made ourselves perfectly understood, we would have left them all Christians. All this we gave them to understand as clearly as possible, and since then, when the sun rose, with great shout

[53]The acquiring of six Indian languages in the course of eight years, through practice imposed by necessity, is not impossible.

ing they would lift their clasped hands to Heaven and then pass them all over their body. The same they did at sunset. They are well conditioned people, apt to follow any line which is well traced for them.

In the village where they had given us the emeralds, they also gave Dorantes over six hundred hearts of deer, opened, of which they kept always a great store for eating. For this reason we gave to their settlement the name of "village of the hearts." Through it leads the pass into many provinces near the South Sea, and any one who should attempt to get there by another route must surely be lost, as there is no maize on the coast, and they eat powdered fox-tail grass, straw, and fish, which they catch in the sea in rafts, for they have no canoes. The women cover their loins with straw and grass. They are a very shy and surly people.

We believe that, near the coast, in a line with the villages which we followed, there are more than a thousand leagues of inhabited land, where they have plenty of victuals, since they raise three crops of beans and maize in the year. There are three kinds of deer, one kind as large as calves are in Castilla. The houses in which they live are huts. They have a poison, from certain trees of the size of our apple trees. They need but pick the fruit and rub their arrows with it; and if there is no fruit they take a branch and with its milky sap do the same. Many of those trees are so poisonous that if the leaves are pounded and washed in water near by, the deer, or any other animal that drinks of it burst at once.[54] In this village we stayed three days, and at a day's journey from it was another one, where such a rain overtook us that, as the river rose high, we could not cross it, and remained there fifteen days.

During this time Castillo saw, on the neck of an Indian, a little buckle from a sword-belt, and in it was sewed a horseshoe nail. He took it from the Indian, and we asked

[54]Not in the report given by Oviedo, but mentioned by him as from the edition of 1542 (p. 618). The village of the "hearts" is a point well established in southern central Sonora. (See "The Journey of Coronado," in this series, by Mr. Winship.)

what it was; they said it had come from Heaven. We further asked who had brought it, and they answered that some men, with beards like ours, had come from Heaven to that river; that they had horses, lances and swords, and had lanced two of them.

As cautiously as possible, we then inquired what had become of those men; and they replied they had gone to sea, putting their lances into the water and going into it themselves, and that afterwards they saw them on top of the waves moving towards sunset.

We gave God our Lord many thanks for what we had heard, for we were despairing to ever hear of Christians again. On the other hand, we were in great sorrow and much dejected, lest those people had come by sea for the sake of discovery only. Finally, having such positive notice of them, we hastened onward, always finding more traces of the Christians, and we told the Indians that we were now sure to find the Christians, and would tell them not to kill Indians or make them slaves, nor take them out of their country, or do any other harm, and of that they were very glad.

We travelled over a great part of the country, and found it all deserted, as the people had fled to the mountains, leaving houses and fields out of fear of the Christians. This filled our hearts with sorrow, seeing the land so fertile and beautiful, so full of water and streams, but abandoned and the places burned down, and the people, so thin and wan, fleeing and hiding; and as they did not raise any crops their destitution had become so great that they ate tree-bark and roots. Of this distress we had our share all the way along, because they could provide little for us in their indigence, and it looked as if they were going to die. They brought us blankets, which they had been concealing from the Christians, and gave them to us, and told us how the Christians had penetrated into the country before, and had destroyed and burnt the villages, taking with them half of the men and all the women and children, and how those who could escaped by flight. Seeing them in this plight, afraid to stay anywhere, and that they neither would nor could cultivate the soil, preferring to die rather than suffer such cruelties, while they showed the greatest pleasure at being with us, we began to apprehend that the Indians who were in arms against the Christians might ill-treat us in retaliation for what the Christians did to them. But when it pleased God our Lord to take us to those Indians, they respected and held us precious, as the former had done, and even a little more, at which we were not a little astonished, while it clearly shows how, in order to bring those people to Christianity and obedience unto Your Imperial Majesty, they should be well treated, and not otherwise.

They took us to a village on the crest of a mountain, which can be reached only by a very steep trail, where we found a great many people, who had gathered there out of dread of the Christians. These received us very well, giving us all they had: over two thousand loads of maize, which we distributed among the poor, famished people who had led us to the place. The next day we dispatched (as we were wont to do) four runners, to call together as many as could be reached, to a village three journeys away; and on the next day we followed with all the people that were at the place, always meeting with signs and vestiges where the Christians had slept.

At noon we met our messengers, who told us they had not found anybody, because all were hidden in the woods, lest the Christians might kill or enslave them; also that, on the night before, they had seen the Christians and watched their movements, under cover of some trees, behind which they concealed themselves, and saw the Christians take many Indians along in chains. At this the people who were with us became frightened, and some turned back to give the alarm through the land that Christians were coming, and many more would have done the same had we not told them to stay and have no fear, at which they quieted down and were comforted. We had Indians with us at the time who came from a distance of a hundred leagues, and whom we could not induce to go back to their homes. So, in order to reassure them, we slept there that night, and the next day went further, and slept on the road; and the day after those we had sent to explore guided us to where they had seen the Christians. Reaching the place in the evening, we clearly saw they had told the truth, and also, from the stakes to which the horses had been tied, that there were horsemen among them.

From here, which is called the river of Petutan,[55] to the river which Diego de Guzman reached, there may be, from the place where we first heard of the Christians, eighty leagues; thence to the village where the rain overtook us, twelve leagues; and from there to the South Sea twelve leagues.[56] Throughout all that country, wherever it is mountainous, we saw many signs of gold, antimony, iron, copper and other metals. Where the permanent houses are it is so hot that even in January the air is very warm. From there to the southward the land, which is uninhabited as far as the Sea of the North, is very barren and poor. There we suffered great and almost incredible starvation; and

[55]Petlatlan.

[56]The distances must, of course, be taken with due reserve.

those who roam through that country and dwell in it are very cruel people, of evil inclinations and habits. The Indians who live in permanent houses and those in the rear of them pay no attention to gold nor silver, nor have they any use for either of these metals.

Having seen positive traces of Christians and become satisfied they were very near, we gave many thanks to our Lord for redeeming us from our sad and gloomy condition. Any one can imagine our delight when he reflects how long we had been in that land, and how many dangers and hardships we had suffered. That night I entreated one of my companions to go after the Christians, who were moving through the part of the country pacified and quieted by us, and who were three days ahead of where we were. They did not like my suggestion, and excused themselves from going, on the ground of being tired and worn out, although any of them might have done it far better than I, being younger and stronger.

Seeing their reluctance, in the morning I took with me the negro and eleven Indians and, following the trail, went in search of the Christians. On that day we made ten leagues, passing three places were they had slept. The next morning I came upon four Christians on horseback, who, seeing me in such a strange attire, and in company with Indians, were greatly startled. They stared at me for quite awhile, speechless; so great was their surprise that they could not find words to ask me anything. I spoke first, and told them to lead me to their captain, and we went together to Diego de Alcaraz, their commander.[57]

After I had addressed him he said that he was himself in a plight, as for many days he had been unable to capture Indians, and did not know where to go, also that starvation was beginning to place them in great distress. I stated to him that, in the rear

[57]He was an officer of Nuño de Guzman, and a worthy one, at that, trained in the school of arbitrariness and cruelty of his commander. Oviedo (III, p. 612) says that there were twenty Spaniards on horseback, according to the report to the Audiencia.

of me, at a distance of ten leagues, were Dorantes and Castillo, with many people who had guided us through the country. He at once dispatched three horsemen, with fifty of his Indians, and the negro went with them as guide, while I remained and asked them to give me a certified statement of the date—year, month and day—when I had met them, also the condition in which I had come, with which request they complied.

From this river to the village called San Miguel, which pertains to the government called New Galicia, there are thirty leagues.

Five days later Andrés Dorantes and Alonso del Castillo came with those who had gone in quest of them. They brought along more than six hundred Indians, from the village, the people of which the Christians had caused to flee to the woods, and who were in hiding about the country. Those who had come with us as far as that place had taken them cut of their places of concealment, turning them over to the

Christians. They had also dispatched the others who had come that far.

When they arrived at where I was Alcaraz begged me to send for the people of the villages along the banks of the river, who were hiding in the timber, and he also requested me to order them to fetch supplies. There was no occasion for the latter, as the Indians always took good care to bring us whatever they could; nevertheless, we sent our messengers at once to call them, and six hundred persons came with all the maize they had, in pots closed with clay, which they had buried for concealment. They also brought nearly everything else they possessed, but we only took of the food, giving the rest to the Christians for distribution among themselves.

Thereupon we had many and bitter quarrels with the Christians, for they wanted to make slaves of our Indians, and we grew so angry at it that at our departure we forgot to take along many bows, pouches and arrows, also the five emeralds, and so they were left and lost to us. We gave the Christians a great many cow-skin robes, and other objects, and had much trouble in persuading the Indians to return home and plant their crops in peace. They insisted upon accompanying us until, according to their custom, we should be in the custody of other Indians, because otherwise they were afraid to die; besides, as long as we were with them, they had no fear of the Christians and of their lances. At all this the Christians were greatly vexed, and told their own interpreter to say to the Indians how we were of their own race, but had gone astray for a long while, and were people of no luck and little heart, whereas they were the lords of the land, whom they should obey and serve.

The Indians gave all that talk of theirs little attention. They parleyed among themselves, saying that the Christians lied, for we had come from sunrise, while the others came from where the sun sets; that we cured the sick, while the others killed those who were healthy; that we went naked and shoeless, whereas the others wore clothes and went on horseback and with lances. Also, that we asked for nothing, but gave away all we were presented with, meanwhile the others seemed to have no other aim than to steal what they could, and never gave anything to anybody. In short, they recalled all our deeds, and praised them highly, contrasting them with the conduct of the others.

This they told the interpreter of the Christians, and made understood to the others by means of a language they have among them, and by which we understood each other. We call those who use that language properly *Primahaitu,* which means the same as saying Bizcayans. For more than four hundred leagues, of those we travelled, we found this language in use, and the only one among them over that extent of country.[58] Finally, we never could convince the Indians that we belonged to the other Christians, and only with much trouble and insistency could we prevail upon them to go home.

We recommended to them to rest easy and settle again in their villages, tilling and

[58]No mention of such an idiom in Oviedo, and I do not venture any suggestion as to what language it might have been. The references to the Basque language may mean that it was as difficult to understand as that idiom.

planting their fields as usual, which, from lying waste, were overgrown with shrubbery, while it is beyond all doubt the best land in these Indies, the most fertile and productive of food, where they raise three crops every year. It has an abundance of fruit, very handsome rivers, and other waters of good virtues. There are many evidences and traces of gold and silver; the inhabitants are well conditioned, and willingly attend to the Christians, that is, those of the natives that are friendly. They are much better inclined than the natives of Mexico; in short, it is a country that lacks nothing to make it very good. When the Indians took leave of us they said they would do as we had told them, and settle in their villages, provided the Christians would not interfere, and so I say and affirm that, if they should not do it, it will be the fault of the Christians.

After we had dispatched the Indians in peace, and with thanks for what they had gone through with and for us, the Christians (out of mistrust) sent us to a certain Alcalde Cebreros, who had with him two other men.[59] He took us through forests and uninhabited country in order to prevent our communicating with the Indians, in reality, also, to prevent us from seeing or hearing what the Christians were carrying on.

This clearly shows how the designs of men sometimes miscarry. We went on with the idea of insuring the liberty of the Indians, and, when we believed it to be assured, the opposite took place. The Spaniards had planned to fall upon those Indians we had sent back in fancied security and in peace, and that plan they carried out.

They took us through the timber for two days, with no trail, bewildered and without water, so we all expected to die from thirst. Seven of our men perished, and many friends whom the Christians had taken along[60] could not reach before noon the following day the place, where we found water that same night. We travelled with them

[59]Cebreros was another of Guzman's followers and disciples, as far as treatment of the Indians was concerned.

[60]This passage, like many others, is quite obscure. The term friends (*"amigos"*) seems to indicate as if the Spaniards had had in their company friendly Indians who assisted them in their slave-hunting enterprise.

twenty-five leagues, more or less, and at last came to a settlement of peaceable Indians. There the Alcalde left us and went ahead, three leagues further, to a place called Culiacan, where Melchor Diaz was chief Alcalde and the captain of the province.[61]

As soon as the chief Alcalde became informed of our arrival, on the same night he came to where we were. He was deeply moved, and praised God for having delivered us in His great pity. He spoke to us and treated us very well, tendering us, in his name, and in behalf of the Governor, Nuño de Guzman, all he had and whatever he might be able to do. He appeared much grieved at the bad reception and evil treatment we had met at the hands of Alcaraz and the others, and we verily believe that, had *he* been there at the time, the things done to us and the Indians would not have occurred.

[61]For Melchor Diaz and his career, see "The Journey of Coronado." He was entirely different from Alcaraz and Cebreros, and of uncommon ability and energy, while at the same time cautious and humane.

Passing the night there, we were about to leave in the morning of the next day, but the chief Alcalde entreated us to stay. He said that by remaining we would render a great service to God and to Your Majesty, as the country was depopulated, lying waste, and well nigh destroyed. That the Indians were hiding in the woods, refusing to come out and settle again in their villages. He suggested that we should have them sent for, and urge them, in the name of God and of Your Majesty, to return to the plain and cultivate the soil again.

This struck us as difficult of execution. We had none of our Indians with us, nor any of those who usually accompanied us and understood such matters. At last we ventured to select two Indians from among those held there as captives, and who were from that part of the country. These had been with the Christians whom we first met, and had seen the people that came in our company, and knew, through the latter, of the great power and authority we exercised all through the land, the miracles we had worked, the cures we had performed, and many other particulars. With these Indians we sent others from the village, to jointly call those who had taken refuge in the mountains, as well as those from the river of Petlatlan, where we had met the Christians first, and tell them to come, as we wished to talk to them. In order to insure their coming, we gave the messengers one of the large gourds we had carried in our hands (which were our chief insignia and tokens of great power).

Thus provided and instructed, they left and were absent seven days. Then they came back, and with them three chiefs of those who had been in the mountains, and with these were fifteen men. They presented us with beads, turquoises, and feathers, and the messengers said the people from the river whence we had started could not be found, as the Christians had again driven them into the wilderness.

Melchor Diaz told the interpreter to speak to the Indians in our name and say that he came in the name of *God,* Who is in heaven, and that we had travelled the world over for many years, telling all the people we met to believe in God and serve Him, for *He* was the Lord of everything upon earth, Who rewarded the good, whereas to the bad ones He meted out eternal punishment of fire. That when the good ones died He took them up to heaven, where all lived forever and there was neither hunger nor thirst, nor any other wants—only the greatest imaginable glory. But that those who would not believe in *Him* nor obey *His* commandments he thrust into a huge fire beneath the earth and into the company of demons, where the fire never went out, but tormented them forever. Moreover, he said that if they became Christians and served *God* in the manner we directed, the Christians would look upon them as brethren and treat them very well, while we would command that no harm should be done to them; neither should they be taken out of their country, and the Christians would become their great friends. If they refused to do so, then the Christians would ill treat them and carry them away into slavery.

To this they replied, through the interpreter, that they would be very good Christians and serve God.

Upon being asked whom they worshipped and to whom they offered sacrifices, to whom they prayed for health and water for the fields, they said, to a man in Heaven. We asked what was his name, and they said *Aguar,* and that they believed he had created the world and everything in it.

We again asked how they came to know this, and they said their fathers and grandfathers had told them, and they had known it for a very long time; that water and all good things came from him. We explained that this being of whom they spoke was the same we called God, and that thereafter they should give Him that name and worship and serve *Him* as we commanded, when they would fare very well.

They replied that they understood us thoroughly and would do as we had told.

So we bade them come out of the mountains and be at ease, peaceable, and settle the land again, rebuilding their houses. Among these houses they should rear one to God, placing at its entrance a cross like the one we had, and when Christians came, they should go out to receive them with crosses in their hands, in place of bows and other weapons, and take the Christians to their homes, giving them to eat of what they had. If they did so, the Christians would do them no harm, but be their friends.

They promised to do as we ordered, and the captain gave them blankets, treating them handsomely, and they went away, taking along the two captives that had acted as our messengers.

This took place in presence of a scribe (notary) and of a great many witnesses.

As soon as the Indians had left for their homes and the people of that province got news of what had taken place with us, they, being friends of the Christians, came to see us, bringing beads and feathers. We ordered them to build churches and put crosses in them, which until then they had not done. We also sent for the children of the chiefs to be baptized, and then the captain pledged himself before *God* not to make any raid, or allow any to be made, or slaves captured from the people and in the country we had set at peace again. This vow he promised to keep and fulfil so long until His Majesty and the Governor, Nuño de Guzman, or the Viceroy, in his name, would ordain something else better adapted to the service of God and of His Majesty.

After baptizing the children we left for the village of San Miguel, where, on our arrival, Indians came and told how many people were coming down from the mountains, settling on the plain, building churches and erecting crosses; in short, complying with what we had sent them word to do. Day after day we were getting news of how all was being done and completed.

Fifteen days after our arrival Alcaraz came in with the Christians who had been raiding, and they told the captain how the Indians had descended from the mountains and settled on the plain; also that villages formerly deserted were now well populated, and how the Indians had come out to receive them with crosses in their hands, had taken them to their houses, giving them of what they had, and how they slept the night there. Amazed at these changes and at the sayings of the Indians who said they felt secure, he ordered that no harm be done to them, and with this they departed.—May *God* in *His* infinite mercy grant that in the days of Your Majesty and under your power and sway, these people become willingly and sincerely subjects of the true Lord Who created and redeemed them. We believe they will be, and that Your Majesty is destined to bring it about, as it will not be at all difficult.[62]

For two thousand leagues did we travel, on land, and by sea in barges, besides ten months more after our rescue from captivity; untiringly did we walk across the land, but nowhere did we meet either sacrifices or idolatry. During all that time we crossed from one ocean to the other, and from what we very carefully ascertained there may be, from one coast to the other and across the greatest width, two hundred leagues.[63] We

[62]The substance of the foregoing is in Oviedo, but most details are omitted. (Compare pp. 612 to 614.)

[63]There are manifest misprints in the distances, but they exist in both editions, 1542 and 1555.

heard that on the shores of the South there are pearls and great wealth, and that the richest and best is near there.

At the village of San Miguel we remained until after the fifteenth of May, because from there to the town of Compostela—where the Governor, Nuño de Guzman, resided—there are one hundred leagues of deserted country threatened by hostiles, and we had to take an escort along. There went with us twenty horsemen, accompanying us as many as forty leagues; afterwards we had with us six Christians, who escorted five hundred Indian captives. When we reached Compostela, the Governor received us very well, giving us of what he had, for us to dress in; but for many days I could bear no clothing, nor could we sleep, except on the bare floor. Ten or twelve days later we left for Mexico. On the whole trip we were well treated by the Christians; many came to see us on the road, praising God for having freed us from so many dangers. We reached Mexico on Sunday, the day before the vespers of Saint James, and were very well received by the Viceroy and the

Marquis of the Valley, who presented us with clothing, offering all they had. On the day of Saint James there was a festival, with bull-fight and tournament.

After taking two months' rest at Mexico I desired to come over to this realm, but when ready to sail in October, a storm wrecked the vessel and it was lost. So I determined to wait until winter would be over, as in these parts navigation is then very dangerous on account of storms.

When winter was past, Andrés Dorantes and I left Mexico, during Lent, for Vera Cruz, to take a ship there, but had again to wait for favorable winds until Palm Sunday. We embarked and were on board more than fifteen days, unable to leave on account of a calm, and the vessel began to fill with water. I took passage on one of the ships which were in condition to leave, while Dorantes remained on the first one,[64] and on the tenth day of the month three craft left port.

We navigated together for one hundred

[64]This explains why Dorantes remained in Mexico, where he afterwards attempted to set on foot an expedition to the North, but failed.

and fifty leagues; afterwards two of the ships dropped behind, and in the course of a night we lost track of them. It seems that, as we found out later, their pilots and skippers did not venture any further, and returned to port without giving us any warning; neither did we hear any more from them. So we kept on, and on the fourth of May reached the port of Habana, on the Island of Cuba, where we waited until the second of June, still hoping for the other two vessels to arrive. Then we left.

We were afraid of falling in with French craft that only a few days before had captured three of ours.

At the altitude of the Island of Bermuda a storm overtook us, as is quite usual in those parts—according to the people who are wont to travel in them—and for a whole night we considered ourselves lost. But it pleased God that, when morning came, the storm abated and we could proceed on our way. Twenty-nine days after sailing from Habana we had made eleven hundred leagues, said to be the distance from it to the settlement of the Azores, and the next day we passed the island called of the raven,[65] and met with a French vessel at noon. She began to follow us, having with her a caravel taken from the Portuguese, and gave us chase. That same evening we saw nine more sail, but at such a distance that we could not distinguish whether they were of the same nation as our pursuer, or Portuguese. At nightfall the Frenchman was but a cannon-shot from our ship, and as soon as it was dark we changed our course so as to get away from him. As he was close upon us he saw our manœuvre and did the same, and this happened three or four times.

The Frenchman could have taken us then, but he preferred to wait until daylight. It pleased God that, when morning came, we found ourselves, as well as the French ship, surrounded by the nine craft we had seen the evening before, and which turned out to belong to the Portuguese navy. I thank Our Lord for having allowed me to escape from peril on land and sea.

[65]Corvo, one of the Azores; northwestern group.

When the French saw it was the fleet of Portugal they released the caravel, which was filled with negroes. They had taken it along in order to make us believe they were Portuguese and to induce us to expect them. On separating from the caravel the Frenchman told the skipper and pilot we were French also, belonging to their own navy; then they put into their vessel sixty oarsmen, and thus, by oar and sail, went away with incredible swiftness.

The caravel then approached the galley warning its captain that both our vessel and the other were French, so that when we came up to the galley and the squadron saw it, believing us to be French, they cleared for action and came to attack us. But when we were near enough to them we saluted, and they saw we were friends. They had been deceived, suffering the privateer to escape by means of his strategy in telling that we were also French. Four caravels went in pursuit of him. Having come up with the galley and presented our respects, the captain, Diego de Silveira, asked where we came from and what we had on board. We told him from New Spain, and that we carried silver and gold. He inquired how much it might be, and the skipper informed him that we had about three hundred thousand Castellanos. Thereupon the captain exclaimed: "Faith, you come back very rich, although you have a bad craft and miserable artillery. That dog of a French renegade has lost a fat morsel, the bastard! Now, go ahead, since you escaped; follow me closely, and, God helping, I shall lead you back to Spain."

The caravels that had gone in pursuit of the French soon returned because the latter sailed too fast for them and they did not want to leave their squadron, which was escorting three ships loaded with spices.

We reached the Island of Tercera,[63] where we rested fifteen days and took in supplies, also waiting for another ship from India, with the same kind of cargo as the three our fleet was escorting. At the end of the fifteen days we sailed, all together, for the port of Lisbon, where we arrived

[63]Terceira, another of the Azores; central group.

on the ninth of August, vespers of Saint Laurentius day, of the year 1537.

And, in Testimony of, that what I have stated in the foregoing narrative is true, I hereunto sign my name:

CABEZA de VACA.

The document which this is taken from was signed with his name and bore the seal with his coat of arms.

Since, in the foregoing narrative, I have related the Journey, the arrival at, and the departure from, the country, and return to this realm, I now wish to tell also what happened to the ships and to the people who remained on board of them. I have not said anything about them as yet, for the reason that we heard nothing of their fate until after our return, when we found many of the survivors in New Spain and some here in Castile, through whom we learned everything that occurred to them after we had forsaken the three vessels, one having been lost previously on the wild coast.

These vessels were in great peril, and had on board a hundred persons with few supplies. Among these people were ten married women, one of whom had foretold the Governor many things that afterwards happened to him.

When he marched inland she warned him not to go, as neither he nor any of his company would return, and that, should any come back, God would work miracles through him, as she felt sure that few, or none, would escape. The Governor retorted that he and all who went with him expected to fight and conquer many and very strange people and countries, so that, while many would have to die in the conquest, he was sure, from the accounts he had of the richness of the country, that the survivors would be fortunate and become very wealthy. He entreated the woman to tell him who it was that had acquainted her with the things, past and present, of which she had spoken. She answered that in Castile a Moorish woman from Hornachos had told her what she said to us before we left there, all of which took place as predicted.

After the Governor had appointed for his lieutenant and commander of all the vessels and their crews one Carvallo, a native of Cuenca de Huete, we marched off, the Governor leaving orders that they embark at once and proceed to Pánuco, hugging the coast always and keeping a lookout for the port where, when found, they should wait for us.

At the time the people were embarking, some saw, and distinctly overheard, the woman before mentioned saying to the other women that, since their husbands had gone inland to affront such imminent peril, they should not think of them any longer, but at once look for other husbands; that she was going to do it, for her part. So she and the others married, and lived with those that were on board the vessels.

The vessels set sail and went on, but did not find the port in the direction they were proceeding, so they turned around and went back where, five leagues further down from our landing-place, they struck the harbor. It stretched inland for seven or eight leagues and was the one we had already discovered and where we had found the boxes from Spain, as told before, and where were the bodies of Christians. From this harbor and along that coast the three vessels, together with one that rejoined them from Habana and the brigantine, cruised in search of us for nearly a year, and then, not finding us, they went to New Spain.

That harbor is the best on earth. It sweeps inland for seven or eight leagues; the water is six fathoms deep at the mouth and five near the shore; the bottom is mud, and there are no tides inside the bay, nor heavy storms. There is space in it for many vessels, and it has many fish. The distance from it to Habana, a Christian town on Cuba, is one hundred leagues on a line from north to south. The breezes are constant, and the trip is made from one place to the other in four days, because the vessels go and come with little trouble.

And now that I have given an account of the ships, it may be well to record also who those are and where from, whom it pleased God to rescue from all these dangers and hardship. The first is Alonso del Castillo

Maldonado, a native of Salamanca and son of Doctor Castillo and Doña Aldonza Maldonado. The second is Andrés Dorantes, son of Pablo Dorantes, born at Béjar, but a resident of Gibraléon. The third is Alvar Nuñez Cabeza de Vaca, son of Francisco de Vera and grandson of Pedro de Vera, who conquered the Canarian Islands. His mother was called Doña Teresa Cabeza de Vaca, and she was a native of Xerez de la Frontera. The fourth was Estévanico, an Arab negro from Azamor,

y nieto de Pedro de Vera el que gano a Canaria: y su madre se llamaua doña Teresa cabeça de vaca natural de Xerez dela frontera. El quarto se llama Esteuanico es negro Alarabe natural de Azamor.:.

Fin.:.

Fue impresso el presente tratado enla magnifica, noble, y antiquissima ciudad de Zamora: por los honrrados varones Augustin de paz y Juan Picardo compañeros impressores de libros vezinos dela dicha ciudad. A costa y espensas del virtuoso varon Juan pedro musetti mercader de libros vezino de Medina del campo. Acabose en seys dias del mes de Octubre. Año del nascimiento d nro saluador Jesu Cristo de mil y quinientos y quarenta y dos Años.

1542

COLOPHON OF EDITION OF 1542.
Reduced from original in Lenox Branch of N. Y. Public Library.

LETTER OF MENDOZA AND REPORT OF FATHER MARCOS OF NIZZA.—INTRODUCTORY NOTE.

IN order to furnish the reader the available data concerning the fate of the two companions of Cabeza de Vaca, who remained in Mexico after his return to Spain, it has been deemed proper to add the two documents which follow. There is first a letter of the Viceroy Don Antonio de Mendoza in which, as far as I am able to ascertain, the only (very meagre) data concerning the subsequent career of Andrés Dorantes in America are found. This is followed by the well-known report of Father Marcos of Nizza on his expedition to Cibola (Zuñi), in which the Moor Estévanico acted as his guide and perished. The text of the documents is taken from the edition of 1810 of "Hackluyt's Collection of the Early Voyages, Travels, and Discoveries of the English Nation," Vol. III., pp. 436 to 4446. The translation is known to be quite indifferent, still the main points are reliable and it fully serves the purpose, which is not to furnish a critical study of Father Marcos of Nizza, and his achievements, but simply to supply the information indicated, and, at the same time, establish the logical connection of this narrative with the "Journey of Coronado," already presented in "The Trail-Makers."

AD. F. BANDELIER.

A LETTER WRITTEN BY THE MOST HONORABLE LORD DON ANTONIO DE MENDOZA, VICE-ROY OF NUEVA ESPANNA, TO THE EMPERORS MAIESTIE.

Of Certaine Noblemen Which Sought to Discover the End of the Firme Land of Nueva Espanna Toward the North. The Arrivall of Vazquez de Coronado with Frier Marco at S. Michael of Culiacan, with Commission to the Governors of Those Partes, to Pacifie the Indians, anl Not to Make Them Slaves Any More.

IN the ships that went last from hence (whereof Michael de Usnago was Admiral) I wrote into your maiestie, how I had sent two Franciscan Friers to discover the end of this firme land, which stretcheth to the North. And because their iourney fell out to greater purpose than was looked for, I will declare the whole matter from the beginning. It may please your Maiestie to call to mind how often I wrote unto your Highnesse, that I desired to know the ende of this Province of Nueva Espanna, because it is so great a countrey, and that we have yet no knowledge thereof. Neither had I onely this desire; for Nunno de Guzman departed out of this city of Mexico with 400 horsemen, and 14,000 Indians footemen borne in these Indias, being the best men and the best furnished, which have bene seene in these parts; and he did so little with them, that the most part of them were consumed in the enterprize and could not enter nor discover any more then already was discovered. After this the saide Nunno Guzman beeing Governour of Nueva Galicia, sent Captaines and Horsemen foorth divers times, which sped no better then he had done. Likewise the Marques de valle Hernando Cortez sent a captaine with 2 ships to discover the coast: which 2 ships and the captaine perished. After that he sent again 2 other ships, one of the which was divided from her consort, and the master and certaine mariners slue the captaine and usurped over the ship.

After this they came to an Island, where the Master with certaine mariners going on land, the Indians of the Country slew them, and tooke their boat: and the ship with those that were in it, returned to the coast of Nueva Galicia, where it ran on ground. By the men which came home in this ship, the Marques had knowledge of the countrey which they had discovered: and then, either for the discontentment which hee had with the bishop of Saint Domingo and with the Judges of this royal audience in Mexico, or rather because of his so prosperous successe in all things here in Nueva Espanna, without seeking any farther intelligence of the state of that Island, he set forward on that voyage with 3 ships, and with certaine footemen and horsemen, not throughly furnished with things necessary; which fell out so contrary to his expectations that the most part of the people which he carried with him, dyed of hunger. And although he had ships, and a Countrey very neere him abounding with victuals, yet could hee never finde meanes to conquer it, but rather it seemed, that God miraculously did hide it from him: and so he returned home without achieving ought else of moment. After this, having heere in my company Andrew Dorantez, which is one of those who were in the voyage of Panphilo Naruaez, I often was in hand with him, supposing that he was able to doe Your Maiestie great service, to imploy him with fortie or fiftie horses, to search out the secret of those parts: and having provided all things necessary for his iourney, and spent much money in that behalfe, the matter was broken off, I wot not how, and that enterprise was given over. Yet of the things which were provided for that purpose, I had left mee a negro, which returned from the foresayde voyage of Naruaez with Dorantez, and certaine slaves which I had bought, and certaine Indians which I had gathered together who were borne in those North partes, whome I sent with Frier Marco de Niça, and his companion a Franciscan Frier, because they had bene long travelled, and exercised in those partes, and had great experience in the affaires of the Indies, and were men of good life and conscience, for whom I obtained leave of their superiours: and so they went with Frances Vazquez de Coronado, governour of Nueva Galicia unto the Citie of Saint Michael of Culiacan, which is the last Province subdued by the Spaniards towarde that quarter, being two hundred leagues distant from this Citie of Mexico. As soone as the governour, and the Friers were come unto that Citie, hee sent certaine of those Indians which I had given him, home into their Countrey, to signifie, and declare to the people of the same, That they were to vnderstand, that your Maiestie had commanded they should not hereafter bee made slaves, and that they should not be afrayd any more, but might returne unto their houses, and live peaceably in them, (for before that time they had bin greatly troubled by the evill dealings which were used toward them) and that your maiestie would cause them to be chastened, which were the causes of their vexation. With these Indians about twentie dayes after returned about 400 men; which coming before the governour said unto him, that they came on the behalfe of al their countrey-men, to tell him, that they desired to see and know those men which did them so great a pleasure as to suffer them to returne to their houses, and to sow maiz for their sustenance, for by the space of many yeres they were driven to flee into the mountaines, hiding themselves like wild beasts, for feare lest they should be made slaves, and that they and all the rest of their people were ready to doe whatsoever should bee commanded them: whom the governour comforted with good wordes, and gave them victuals, and stayed them with him three or foure dayes wherein the Friars taught them to make the signe of the crosse, and to learne the name of our Lorde Jesus

Christ, and they with great diligence sought to learne the same. After these dayes hee sent them home againe, willing them not to be afraid, but to be quiet, giving them apparel, beades, knives, and other such like things, which I had given him for such purposes. The sayde Indians departed very well pleased, and said, that whensoever hee would send for them, they and many others would come to doe whatsoever he would command them. The entrance being thus prepared, Frier Marco and his companion, with the Negro and other slaves, and Indians which I had given him, went forward on their voyage 10 or 12 dayes after. And because I had likewise advertisement of a certaine Province called Topira situate in the mountaines and had appointed the governour Vazquez de Coronado, that he should use meanes to learne the state thereof: he supposing this to be a matter of great moment determined himselfe to goe and search it, having agreed with the said Frier, that he should returne by that part of the mountaine, to meete with him in a certaine valley called Valle de los Coraçones, being 120 leagues distant from Culiacan. The Governour travelling into this province (as I have written in my former letters) found great scarcity of victuals there, and the mountaines so craggy, that he could finde no way to passe forward, and was inforced to returne home to Saint Michael: so that as well in chusing of the entrance, as in not being able to finde the way, it seemeth onto all men that God would shut up the gate to all those, which by strength of humane force have gone about to attempt this enterprise, and hath reveiled it to a poore and bare-footed Frier. And so the Frier beganne to enter into the Land, who because he found his entrance so well prepared, was very well received; and because he wrote the whole successe of his voyage, according to the instruction which I had given him to ondertake the same, I wil not write any more at large, but send your Maiestie this copy of all such things as he observed in the same.

A RELATION OF THE REVEREND FATHER FRIER MARCO DE NICA, TOUCHING HIS DISCOVERY OF THE KINGDOM OF CEUOLA OR CIBOLA, SITUATE ABOUT 30. DEGREES OF LATITUDE, TO THE NORTH OF NUEUA ESPANNA.

CHAPTER I.

Frier Marco de Niça Departeth from Saint Michael in the Province of Culiacan, Standing in 24. Degrees of Northerly Latitude: and Coming to the Towne of Petatlan, Receiveth Many Courtesies of the Indians There. Departing from Thence, He Had Information of Many Islands, and of a Great Countrey Inhabited with Civil People; He Cometh to Vacupa: Where During His Aboad, He Heard Newes of Cevola, and of the State of the 7 Cities, and of Other Provinces, and of the Rich Islands of Perles, which Extend Northward Upon the Coast.

I FRIER MARCO DE NICA of the order of S. Francis, for the execution of the instruction of the right honourable lord Don Antonio de Mendoça, Vice-roy and captaine Generall for the Emperors Maiestie in New Spaine, departed from the towne of S. Michael in the province of Culiacan on Friday the 7. of March, in the yeere 1539. having for my companion Frier Honoratus, and carying with me Stephan a Negro, belonging to Andrew Dorantez, and certaine of those

Indians which the sayde lord Vice-roy had made free, and bought for this purpose: whom Frances Vazquez de Coronado governour of Nueva Galicia delivered me, and with many other Indians of Petatlan, and of the towne called Cuchillo, which is some 50. leagues from Petatlan, who came to the valley of Culiacan, shewing themselves to bee exceeding glad, because they were certified by the Indians which had bin set free, whom the said governour had sent before to advertise them of their libertie, that none of them from thenceforth should be made slaves, and that no man should invade them, nor use them badly; signifying onto them, that the Emperors Maiesty had willed and commanded that it should be so. With the foresaid company I went on my voyage vntil I came to the towne of Petatlan, finding all the way great intertainment, and provision of victuals, with roses, flowers, and other such things, and bowers which they made for me of chalke and boughs platted together in all places where there were no houses. In this towne of Petatlan I rested 3. dayes, because my companion Honoratus fell so sicke, that I was constrained to leave him there behinde.

Then, according to my said instruction, I followed my iourney as the holy Ghost did leade me, without any merit of mine, having in my company the said Stephan the Negro, Dorantez, and certaine of the Indians which had bin set at liberty, and many of the people of the countrey, which gave me great intertainment and welcome in all places where I came, and made mee bowers of trees, giving me such victuals as they had, although they were but small: because (as they said) it had not rained there in 3 yeres, and because the Indians of this countrey sought means rather to hide themselves, then to sowe corne, for feare of the Christians of the Towne of S. Michael, which were wont to make in-roades even to that place, and to warre upon them, and to carry them away captives. In all this way, which may be about 25 or 30. leagues from that part of Petatlan, I saw nothing worthy the noting, save that there came to seeke me certaine Indians from the Island, where Fernando Cortez the Marques of the valley had bin, of whom I was informed, that it was an Island, and not firme land, as some suppose it to be. They came to y[e] firme land upon certaine rafts of wood: and from the maine to the island is but halfe a league by sea, little more or lesse. Likewise certaine Indians of another island greater then this came to visit me, which island is farther off, of whom I was informed that there were 30. other small islands, which were inhabited, but had smal store of victuals, saving 2. which have maiz or corne of the countrey. These Indians had about their necks many great shels which were mother of Pearle. I shewed them pearles which I carryed with me for a shew, and they told me that there were in the Islands great store of them, and those very great: howbeit I saw none of them. I followed my voyage through a desert of 4 dayes iourney, having in my company both the Indians of the islands and those of the mountaines which I had passed, and at the end of this desert I found other indians which marvelled to see me, because they had no knowledge of any Christians, having no traffike nor conversation with those Indians which I had passed, in regard of the great desert which was between them. These Indians intertained me exceeding courteously, and gave me great store of victuals and sought to touch my garments and called me Hagota, which in their language signifieth A man come from heaven. These Indians I advertised by my interpreter, according to my instructions, in the Knowledge of our Lord God in heaven, and of the Emperor. In these countries and in all places els by all wayes and meanes possible, I sought information where any Countreys were of more Cities and people of civilitie and onderstanding, then those which I had found: and I could heare no newes of any such: howbeit they tolde mee, that foure or five dayes iourney within the Countrey, at the foote of the mountaines, there is a large and mightie plaine, wherein they tolde mee, that there were many great Townes, and people clad in Cotton: and when I shewed them certaine metals which I carryed with mee, to learne what riche metals were in the Lande, they tooke the minerall of Golde and tolde mee, that thereof were vesselles among the people of that plaine, and that they carryed certaine round greene stones hanging at their nostrilles, and at their eares, and that they have certaine thinne plates of that Golde, wherewith they scrape off their sweat, and that the walles of their Temples are covered therewith, and that they use it in all their household vessels. And because this Valley is distant from the Sea-coast, and my instruction was not to leave the Coast, I determined to leave the discovery thereof ontill my returne; at which time I might doe it more commodiously.

Thus I travelled three dayes iourney through Townes inhabited by the sayde people, of whome I was received as I was of those which I had passed, and came onto a Towne of reasonable bignesse, called Vacupa, where they shewed mee great courtesies, and gave mee great store of good victuals, because the soyle is very fruitfull, and may bee watered. This Towne is fortie leagues distant from the Sea.

And because I was so farre from the Sea, it being two dayes before Passion Sunday, I determined to stay there until Easter, to informe myselfe of the Islandes, whereof I sayde before that I had information. And so I sent certaine Indians to the Sea by three severall wayes whom I commaunded to bring mee some Indians of the Sea-coast and of some of those Islandes that I might receive information of them: And I sent Stephan Dorantez the Negro another way, whom I commaunded to goe directly northward fiftie or threescore leagues, to see if by that way hee might learne any newes of any notable thing which wee sought to discover, and I agreed with him, that if hee found any knowledge of any peopled and riche countrey which were of great importance, that hee should goe no further but should returne in person, or should sende mee certaine Indians with that token which wee were agreed upon, to wit, that if it were but a meane thing, hee should sende mee a White Crosse of one handfull long; and if it were any great matter, one of two handfuls long; and if it were a Countrey greater and better then Nueva Espanna, hee should send mee a great crosse. So the sayde Stephan departed from mee on Passion-sunday after dinner: and within foure dayes after the messengers of Stephan returned vnto me with a great Crosse as high as a man, and they brought me word from Stephan, that I should forthwith come away after him, for hee had found people which gave him information of a very mighty Province, and that he had certaine Indians in his company, which had bene in the sayd Province, and that he had sent me one of the said Indians. This Indian told me, that it was thirtie dayes iourney from the Towne where Stephan was, vnto the first Citie of the sayde Province, which is called Ceuola. Hee affirmed also that there are seven great Cities in this Province, all vnder one Lord, the houses whereof are made of Lyme & Stone, and are very great, and the least of them with one lofte above head, and some two and of three loftes, and the house of the Lorde of the Province of foure, and that all of them ioyne one onto the other in good order, and that in the gates of the principall houses there are many Turques-stones cunningly wrought, whereof hee sayth they have there great plentie: also that the people of this Citie goe very well apparelled: and that beyond this there are other Provinces, all which (hee sayth) are much greater then these seven cities. I gave credite to his speach because I found him to bee a man of good vnderstanding: but I deferred my departure to follow Stephan Dorantez, both because I thought hee would stay for mee, and also to attend the returne of my messengers which I had sent vnto the Sea, who returned vnto me upon Easter day, bringing with them certaine inhabitants of the Sea-coast, and of two of the Islands. Of whom I vnderstoode, that the Islandes above mentioned were scarce of victuals, as I had learned before, and that they are inhabited by people, which weare shelles of Pearles upon their foreheads, and they say that they have great Pearles, and much Golde. They informed mee of foure and thirtie Islandes, lying one neere vnto another: they say that the people on the sea-coast have small store of victuals, as also those of the Islandes, and that they trafficke one with the other upon raftes. This coast stretcheth northward as is to bee seene. These Indians of the Coast brought me certaine Targets made of Cow-hydes very well dressed, which were so large, that they covered them from the head to the very foote, with a hole in the toppe of the same to looke out before: they are so strong, that a Crossebow (as I suppose) will not pierce them.

CHAPTER II.

He Hath New Information of the Seven Cities by Certaine Indians Called Pintados, and of Three Other Kingdomes Called Marata, Acus, and Totonteac, Being Countreys Very Rich in Turqueses and Hides of Cattel. Following His Voyage Through Those Countries He Taketh Possession Thereof for the Emperors Maiestie, and of the Indians Is Much Honoured and Served with Victuals.

THE same day came three Indians of those which I called Pintados, because I saw their faces, breasts and armes painted. These dwel farther up into the countrey towards the East, and some of them border upon the seven cities, which sayd they came to see mee, because they had heard of mee: and among other things they gave me information of the seven cities, and of the other Provinces, which the Indian that Stephan sent me had tolde mee of, almost in the very same manner that Stephan had sent mee worde; and so I sent backe the people of the sea-coast: and two Indians of the Islands sayde they would goe with mee seven or eight dayes.

So with these and with the three Pintados above mentioned, I departed from Vacupa upon Easter Tuesday, the same way that Stephan went, from whom I received new messengers with a crosse of the bignesse of the first which he sent me: which hastened me forward, and assured me that the land which I sought for, was the greatest and best countrey in all those partes. The sayd messengers told mee particularly without fayling in any one poynt, all that which the first messenger had tolde mee, and much more, and gave mee more plaine information thereof. So I travelled that day being Easter Tuesday, and two dayes more, the very same way that Stephan had gone: at the end of which 3 dayes they tolde mee that from that place a man might travell in thirtie dayes to the citie of Ceuola, which is the first of the seven. Neither did one onely tell me thus much, but very many; who tolde me very particularly of the greatness of the houses, and of the fashion of them, as the first messengers had informed me. Also they told me, that besides these seven Cities, there are 3 other Kingdomes which are called Marata, Acus and Tontonteac. I enquired of them wherefore they travelled so farre from their houses: They said that they went for Turqueses, and Hides of Kine, and other things; and that of all these there was great abundance in this Countrey. Likewise I enquired how, and by what meanes they obtained these things: They tolde me, by their service and by the sweat of their browes, and that they went unto the first citie of the province which is called Ceuola, and that they served them in tilling their ground, and in other businesses, and that they give them Hydes of oxen, which they have in those places, and turqueses for their service, and that the people of this city weare very fine and excellent turqueses hanging at their eares and at their nostrils. They say also, that of these turqueses they make fine workes upon the principall gates of the houses of this citie. They tolde mee, that the apparell which the inhabitants of Ceuola weare, is a gowne of cotten downe to the foote, with a button at the necke, and a long string hanging downe at the same, and that the sleeves of these gownes are as broad beneath as above. They say, they gyrded themselves with gyrdles of turqueses, and that over these coates some weare good apparel, others hides of Kine very well dressed, which they take to bee the best apparell of that countrey, whereof they have there great quantitie. Likewise the women goe apparelled, and covered downe to the foote. These Indians gave me very good intertainment, and curiously enquired the day of my departure from Vacupa, that at my returne they might provide me of foode and lodging. They brought certaine sicke folkes before mee, that I might heale them, and sought to touch my apparell, and gave mee certaine cow-hydes so well trimmed and dressed, that by them a man might coniecture that they were wrought by civile people, and all of them affirmed, that they came from Ceuola.

The next day I followed my iourney, and carrying with mee the Pintados, I came to another Village where I was well received by the people of the same: who likewise sought to touch my garments, and gave mee as particular knowledge of the Lande aforesaide, as I had received of those which mette mee before: and also tolde mee, that from that place certaine people were gone with Stephan Dorantez, foure or five dayes iourney. And here I found a great crosse, which Stephan had left mee for a signe, that the newes of the good Countrey increased, and left worde, that with all haste they should send mee away, and that hee would stay for me at the ende of the first Desert that he mette with. Heere I set up two Crosses, and tooke possession according to mine instruction, because that the Countrey seemed better unto mee then that which I had passed, and that I thought it meete to make an acte of possession as farre as that place.

In this maner I travailed five dayes, alwayes finding inhabited places with great hospitalitie and intertainments, and many Turqueses, and Oxe-hides, and the like report concerning the countrey. Heere I understood, that after two dayes iourney I should finde a desert where there is no foode, but that there were certaine gone before to build mee lodgings, and to carrie foode for me: whereupon I hastened my way, hoping to finde Stephan at the ende thereof, because in that place hee had left worde that hee would stay for mee. Before I came to the desert, I mette with a very pleasant Towne, by reason of great store of waters conveighed thither to water the same. Heere I mette with many people both men & women clothed in Cotton, and some covered with oxe-hydes, which generally they take for better apparell then that of cotton.

All the people in this village go in caconados, that is to say, Turquesses hanging at their nostrilles and eares, which Turquesses they call Cacona. Amongst others, the Lord of this Village came unto me; and two of his brethern, very well apparrelled in cotton, who also were in Caconados, each of them having his collar of Turquesses about his necke; and they presented unto mee many wild beastes, as conies, quailes, Maiz nuttes of Pine trees, and all in great abundance, and offered me many Turqueses, and dressed Oxe-hydes, and very fayre vessels to drinke in, and other things; whereof I would receive no whit. And having my garment of gray cloth, which in Spaine is called çaragoça, the Lord of this Village and the other Indians touched my gowne with their handes, and tolde mee, that of such cloth there was great store in Tontonteac, and that the people of that Countrey wore the same. Whereat I laughed, and sayde that it was nothing else but such apparell of Cotton as they wore. And they replyed: We would have thee thinke that we vnderstand, that that apparell which thou wearest, and that which we weare are of divers sortes. Understand thou, that in Ceulo all the houses are full of that apparrell which we weare, but in Totonteac there are certaine litle beasts, from whom they take that thing wherewith such apparell as thou wearest is made. I prayed them to informe mee more playnely of this matter. And they tolde mee that the sayde beastes were about the bignesses of the two braches or spaniels which Stephan caryed with him, and they say that there is great store of that cattell in Totonteac.

CHAPTER III.

He Entreth into a Desert, and the Indians Suffer Him to Want Nothing Necessary. Following His Voyage, He Commeth into a Fertile Valley, and Hath Certaine Knowledge Given Him (as He Had Before) of the State of Ceuola, and of Totonteac; and That the Coast of the Sea in 35. Degrees Trendeth Much to the Westward; and Also the Kingdomes of Mavata and Acus.

THE next day I entered into the Desert, and where I was to dine, I found bowers made, and victuals in abundance by a rivers side: and at night I found bowers and victuals in like sort, and after that maner I found for 4 dayes travell: all which time the wildernesse continueth.

At the ende of these foure dayes, I entred into a valley very well inhabited with people. At the first village there mette me many men and women with victuals and all of them had Turqueses hanging at their nostrils and eares, and some had collars of turqueses like those which the Lord of the Village before I came to the Desert, and his two brethern wore: saving that they ware them but single about their neckes, and these people weare them three or foure times double, and goe in good apparrell, and skinnes of Oxen: and the women weare of the said Turqueses at their nostrils and eares, and very good wast-coates and other garments. Heere there was as great Knowledge of Ceula, as in Nueva Espanna of Temistitan, and in Peru of Cuzco; and they tolde us particularly the maner of their houses, lodgings, streetes and market-places, as men that had bene oftentimes there, and as those which were furnished from thence with things necessary for the service of their householde, as those also had done, which I already had passed. I told them it was impossible that the houses should be made in such sort as they informed mee, and they for my better vnderstanding tooke earth or ashes, and poured water thereupon, and shewed me how they layd stones upon it, and how the buylding grewe up, as they continued laying stones thereon, vntill it mounted aloft. I asked them whether the men of that countrey had wings to mount up unto those loftes; whereat they laughed, and showed mee a Ladder in as good sort as I myselfe was able to describe it. Then they tooke a Staffe and helde it over their heads, and said that the lofts were so high one above another. Likewise heere I had information of the woollen cloth of Totonteac, where they say are houses like those of Ceuola, and better and more in number, and that it is a great Province, and hath no governour. Here I onderstood that the coast of the sea trended much toward the West; for vnto the entrance of this first desert which I passed, the coast still stretched Northward; and because the trending of the coast is a thing of great importance, I was desirous to Knowe and see it; and I saw plainely, that in 35. degrees the coast stretcheth to the West, whereat I reioyced no lesse, then of the good newes within land, and so I returned back to proceede on my iourney.

Through the foresayd valley I travailed five dayes iourney, which is inhabited with goodly people, and so aboundeth with victuals, that it sufficieth to feede above three thousand horsemen: it is all well watered and like a garden: the burroughs and townes are halfe and a quarter of a league long, and in all these villages, I found very ample report of Ceuola, whereof they made such particular relation onto me, as people which go yeerely thither to earne their living. Here I found a man borne in Ceuola, who told me that he came thither, having escaped from the governour or Lieutenant of the towne; for the Lord of these seven Cities liveth and abideth in one of those townes called Ahacus, and in the rest he appoynteth lieu-tenants under him. This townesman of Ceuola is a white man of a good complexion, somewhat well in yeeres, and of fame greater capacitie then the inhabitants of this valley, or then those which I had left behind me. Hee sayde that hee would goe with mee, that I might begge his pardon: and of him I learned many particulars: he tolde me that Ceuola was a great Citie, inhabited with great store of people, and having many streetes and market-places: and that in some parts of this Citie there are certaine very great houses of five stories high, wherein the chiefe of the Citie assemble themselves at certaine dayes of the yeere. He sayeth that the houses are of Lyme and Stone, according as others had tolde mee before, and that the gates, and small pillars of the principall houses are of Turqueses, and all the vessels wherein they are served, and the other ornaments of their houses were of golde: and that the other sixe Cities are built like onto this, whereof some are bigger: and that Ahacus is the chiefest of them. Hee sayth that toward the Southeast there is a Kingdome called Marata, and that there were woont to be many, and those great Cities, which were all built of houses of Stone, with divers lofts: and that these have and doe wage warre with the Lord of the seven Cities, through which warre this Kingdome of Marata is for the most part wasted, although it yet continueth and maintaineth warre against the other.

Likewise he saith, that the Kingdome called Totonteac lyeth toward the West, which he saith is a very mightie Province, replenished with infinite store of people and riches. And that in the sayde Kingdome they weare woollen cloth like that which I weare, and other finer sorts of woollen cloth made of the fleeces of those beastes which they described before onto me: and that they are a very civile people. Moreover hee tolde me, that there is another great Province and Kingdome called Acus; for there is Acus, and Ahacus with an aspiration, which is the principall of the seven cities: and Acus without an aspiration is a Kingdome and Province of it selfe. He told me also, that the apparrel which they weare in Ceuola is after the same maner as they before had certified me, and that all the inhabitants of the Citie lie upon beddes raysed a good height from the ground, with quilts and canopies over them, which cover the sayde Beds: and hee tolde mee that hee would goe with me to Ceuola and farther also, if I would take him with me. The like relation was given vnto me in this towne by many others, but not so particularly. I travelled three dayes iourney through this valley: the inhabitants whereof made me exceeding great cheere and intertainment. In this valley I saw above a thousand Oxe-hides most excellently trimmed and dressed. And here also I saw farre greater store of Turqueses and chaines made thereof, then in all places which I had passed; and they say, that all commeth from the city of Ceuola whereof they have great Knowledge, as also of the Kingdome of Marata and of the Kingdomes of Acus and Totonteac.

CHAPTER IV.

Of a Very Great Beast with One Horne Upon His Fore-head; and of the Courtesies which the Indians Shewed Frier Marcus of Niça, in His Voyage. Also How Cruelly Stephan Dorantez and His Companions Were Used Upon Their Arrivall at Ceuola, by the Lorde Thereof.

HERE they shewed me an hide halfe as bigge againe as the hide of a great oxe, and tolde me that it was the skin of a beast which had but one horne upon his forehead, and that this horne bendeth toward his breast, and that out of the same goeth a point right forward, wherein he hath so great strength, that it will breake any thing how strong so ever it be, if he runne against it, and that there are great store of these beasts in that Countrey. The colour of the hide is of the colour of a great Goat-skin, and the haire is a finger thicke. Here I had messengers from Stephan which brought me word, that by this time he was come to the farthest part of the desert, and that he was very ioyful, because the farther he went, the more perfect Knowledge he had of the greatnesse of the countrey, and sent me word, that since his departure from me, hee never had found the Indians in any lye; for even vnto that very place he had found al in such maner as they had informed him and hoped that he should find the like at his arrivall in the valley which he was going vnto, as he had found in the villages before passed. I set up crosses and used those acts and ceremonies, which were to be done according to my instructions. The inhabitants requested me to stay here three or foure days, because that from this place there were four days iourney vnto the desert, and from the first entrance into the same desert vnto the citie of Ceuola are 15 great dayes iourney more; also that they would provide victuals, for me and other necessaries for that voyage. Likewise they told me, that with Stephan the Negro were gone above 300 men to beare him company, and to carry victuals after him, and that in like sort many of them would go with me to serve me, because they hoped to returne home rich. I thanked them, and willed them to set things in order with speede, and so I rested there three dayes, wherein I always informed my selfe of Ceuola, and of as many other things as I could learne, and called many Indians vnto mee, and examined them severally and all of them agreed in one tale. and told me of the great multitude of people, and of the order of the streetes, of the greatnesse of the houses, and of the strength of the gates, agreeing altogether with that which the rest before had told me. After three dayes many assembled themselves to go with me, 30 of the principal of whom I tooke, being very well apparrelled, and with chaines of turqueses, which some of them weare five or sixe times double, and other people to cary things necessary for them and me, and so set forward on my voyage.

Thus I entred into the second desert on the 9 of May, and travelled the first day by a very broad and beaten way, and we came to diner vnto a water, where the Indians had made provision for me; and at night we came to another water, where I found a house which they had fully made up for me, and another house stood made where Stephan lodged when he passed that way, and many old cottages and many signes of fire which the people had made that travelled to Ceuola by this way. In this sort I travelled 12 dayes iourney being alway well provided of victuals, of wild beasts, Hares, and Partridges of the same colour and tast with those of Spaine although they are not as big, for they be somewhat lesse. Here met us an Indian the sonne of the chiefe man that accompanied mee, which had gone before with Stephan, who came in a great fright, having his face and body all covered with sweat, and shewing exceeding sadnesse in his countenance; and he told mee that a dayes iourney before Stephan came to Ceuola he sent his great mace made of a gourd by his messenges, as he was always woont to send them before him, that hee might knowe in what sort hee came onto them, which gourd has a string of belles upon it, and two feathers one white and another red, in token that he demanded safe conduct, and that he came peaceably. And when they came to Ceuola before the magistrate, which the Lord of the citie had placed there for his Lieutenant, they delivered him the sayde great gourd, who tooke the same in his hands, and after he spyed the belles, in a great rage and fury he cast it to the ground, and willed messengers to get them packing with speed, for he knew well ynough what people they were, and that they should will them in no case to enter into the citie, for if they did hee would put them all to death. The messengers returned and tolde Stephan how things had passed, who answered them that it made no great matter, and would needes proceed on his voyage till he came to the citie of Ceuola: where he found men that would not let him enter into the towne, but shut him into a great house which stoode without the citie, and straightway tooke all things from him which hee carried to truck and barter with them, and certain turqueses, and other things which he had received of the Indians by the way, and they kept him there all that night without giving him meate or drinke, and the next day in the morning this Indian was a thirst, and went out of the house to drinke at a river that was neere at hand, and within a little while after he saw Stephan running away, and the people followed him, and slewe certain of the Indians which went in his company. And when this Indian saw these things, he hid himselfe on the banks of the river, and afterward crossed the high way of the desert. The Indians that went with me bearing these newes began incontinently to lament, and I thought these heavie and bad news would cost mee my life, neither did I feare so much the losse of mine owne life, as that I should not bee able to returne to give information of the greatnesses of that Countrey, where our Lord God might be glorified: and streight way I cut the cords of my budgets which I carried with me ful of merchandise for traffique, which I would not doe till then, nor give anything to any man, and began to divide all that I carried with mee among the principall men, willing them not to be afraid, but to goe forward with me, and so they did. And going on our way, within a dayes iourney of Ceuola wee met two other Indians of those which went with Stephan, which were bloody and wounded in many places: and as soone as they came to us, they which were with me began to make great lamentation. These wounded Indians I asked for Stephan, and they agreeing in all poynts with the first Indian sayd, that after they had put him into the foresayd great house without giving him meat or drinke all that day and all that night, they tooke from Stephan all the things which hee carried with him. The next day when the Sunne was a lance high, Stephan went out of the house, and some of the chiefe men with him, and suddenly came store of people from the citie, whom as soone as hee sawe he began to run away and we likewise, and foorthwith they shot at us and wounded us, and certaine dead men fell upon us, and so we lay till night and durst not stirre, and we heard great rumours in the citie, and saw many men and women keeping watch and ward upon the walles thereof, and after this we could not see Stephan any more, and wee thinke they have shot him to death, as they have done all the rest which went with him, so that none are escaped but we onely.

CHAPTER V.

The Situation and Greatnesse of the Citie of Ceuola, and How Frier Marcus Tooke Possession Thereof and of Other Provinces, Calling the Same The New Kingdomes of S. Francis, and How After His Departure from Thence Being Reserved by God in So Dangerous a Voyage, He Arrived at Compostella in Nueva Galicia.

HAVING considered the former report of the Indians, and the evill meanes which I had to prosecute my voyage as I desired, I thought it not good wilfully to loose my life as Stephan did; and so tolde them, that God would punish those of Ceuola, and that the Viceroy when he should understand what had happened, would send many christians to chastise them: but they would not believe me, for they sayde that no man was able to withstand the power of Ceuola. And herewith I left them, and went aside two or three stones cast, and when I returned I found an Indian of mine which I had brought from Mexico called Marcus, who wept and sayde unto me: Father, these men have consulted to kill us, for they say, that through your and Stephans meanes their fathers are slaine, and that neither man nor woman of them shall remaine unslaine. Then againe I divided among them certaine other things which I had, to appease them, whereupon they were somewhat pacified, albeit they still shewed great griefe for the people which were slaine. I requested some of them to goe to Ceuola, to see if any other Indian were escaped, with intent that they might learne some newes of Stephan; which I could not obtaine at their handes. When I saw this, I sayd unto them, that I purposed to see the citie of Ceuola, whatsoever came of it. They sayde that none of them would goe with me. At the last when they sawe mee resolute, two of the chiefe of them sayde they would goe with me; with whome and with mine Indians and interpreters I followed my way, till I came within sight of Ceuola, which is situate on a plaine at the foote of a round hill, and maketh shew to bee a faire citie, and is better seated then any that I have seene in these partes. The houses are builded in order, according as the Indians told me, all made of stone with divers stories, and flatte roofes, as farre as I could discerne from a mountaine, whither I ascended to viewe the citie. The people are somewhat white, they weare apparell, and lie in beds, their weapons are bowes, they have Emeralds and other iewels, although they esteeme none so much as turqueses wherewith they adorne the walles of the porches of their houses, and their apparell and vessels, and they use them instead of money through all the Countrey. Their apparell is of cotton and Oxe hides, and this is their most commendable and honourable apparell. They use vessels of gold and silver, for they have no other mettall, whereof there is greater use and more abundance then in Peru, and they buy the same for turqueses in the province of the Pintados, where there are sayd to be mines of great abundance. Of other Kingdomes I could not obtaine so particular instruction. Divers times I was tempted to goe thither, because I knewe I could but hazard my life, and that I had offered unto God the first day that I began my iourney: in the ende I began to bee afraid, considering in what danger I should put my selfe, and that if I should dye, the knowledge of this countrey should be lost, which in my iudgement is the greatest and the best that hitherto hath beene discovered: and when I tolde the chief men, what a goodly citie Ceuola seemed unto mee, they answered me that it was the least of the seven cities, and that Totonteac is the greatest and best of them all, because it hath so many houses and people, and there is no ende of them. Having seene the disposition and situation of the place, I thought good to name that countrey El Nueva reyno de San Francisco: in which place I made a great heape of stones by the helpe of the Indians, and on the toppe thereof I set up a small slender crosse because I wanted meanes to make a greater, and sayd that I set up that crosse and heape in the name of the most honourable Lord Don Antonio de Mendoça Viceroy and Captaine generall of Nueva Espanna, for the Emperour our Lord, in token of possession, according to mine instruction. Which possession I sayd that I tooke in that place of all the seven cities, and of the Kingdomes of Totonteac, of Acus, and of Marata. Thus I returned with much more feare then victuals, and went untill I found the people which I had left behind mee, with all the speede that I could make, whome I overtooke in two dayes travell, and went in their company till I had passed the desert, where I was not made so much of as before: for both men and women made great lamentation for the people which were slaine at Ceuola, and with feare I hastened from the people of this valley, and travelled tenne leagues the first day, and so I went daily eight or ten leagues, without staying until I had passed the second desert. And though I were in feare, yet I determined to go to the great plaine, whereof I said before, that I had information, being situate at the foote of the mountaines, and in that place I vnderstoode, that this plaine is inhabited for many dayes iourney toward the East, but I durst not enter into it, considering, that if hereafter wee shoulde inhabite this other countrey of the seven cities, and the kingdomes before mentioned, that then I might better discover the same, without putting my selfe in hazard, and leaue it for this time, that I might give relation of the things which I had now seene. At the entrance of this plaine I sawe but seven Townes onely of a reasonable bignesse, which were a farre off in a lowe valley beeing very greene and a most fruitfull soyle, out of which ranne many Rivers. I was informed that there was much golde in this valley, and that the inhabitants worke it into vessels and thinne plates, wherewith they strike and take off their sweat, and that they are people that will not suffer those of the other side of the plaine to traffique with them, and they could not tell me the cause thereof. Here I set up two crosses, and tooke possession of the plaine and valley in like sort and order, as I did at other places before mentioned. And from thence I returned on my voyage with as much haste as I coulde make, untill I came to the citie of Saint Michael in the province of Culiacan, thinking there to have found Francis Vazquez de Coronado governour of Nueva Galicia, and finding him not there, I proceeded on my iourney till I came to the citie of Compostella, where I found him. I write not here many other particularities, because they are impertinent to this matter: I only report that which I have seene, and which was tolde me concerning the countreys through which I travelled, and of those which I had information of.